CONSTITUTION OF THE UNITED NATIONS

ANALYSIS OF STRUCTURE AND FUNCTION

By

ALF ROSS, L.L.D., Ph.D.

PROFESSOR OF INTERNATIONAL LAW IN
THE UNIVERSITY OF COPENHAGEN

THE LAWBOOK EXCHANGE, LTD.
Clark, New Jersey
2008

ISBN-13: 978-1-58477-891-2
ISBN-10: 1-58477-891-1

Second printing 2009

The quality of this reprint is equivalent to the quality of the original work.

THE LAWBOOK EXCHANGE, LTD.
33 Terminal Avenue
Clark, New Jersey 07066-1321

Please see our website for a selection of our other publications and fine facsimile reprints of classic works of legal history:
www.lawbookexchange.com

Library of Congress Cataloging-in-Publication Data

Ross, Alf, 1899-
Constitution of the United Nations : analysis of structure and function / by Alf Ross.
p. cm.
Originally published: New York : Rinehart, 1950.
Includes bibliographical references and index.
ISBN-13: 978-1-58477-891-2 (cloth : alk. paper)
ISBN-10: 1-58477-891-1 (cloth : alk. paper)
1. United Nations. Charter. 2. International organization. 3. International law. I. United Nations. Charter. II. Title.
KZ4991.R67 2008
341.23'2--dc22 2008003782

Printed in the United States of America on acid-free paper

CONSTITUTION OF THE UNITED NATIONS

ANALYSIS OF STRUCTURE AND FUNCTION

By

ALF ROSS, L.L.D., Ph.D.

PROFESSOR OF INTERNATIONAL LAW IN
THE UNIVERSITY OF COPENHAGEN

NEW YORK
RINEHART & COMPANY
1950

PRINTED IN DENMARK
A. RASMUSSENS BOGTRYKKERI
RINGKJØBING

FOREWORD

Great importance is to be attached to the careful and critical study of the Charter of the United Nations by independent scholars representing the various cultures and diverse legal systems of the world. The present book by Professor Ross is a noteworthy contribution by a distinguished Scandinavian scholar which will be warmly welcomed not only by legal circles but by all who are interested in the serious study of international affairs. The reader will find here a keen analysis of the structure and functions of the Organization, to the interpretation of which Professor Ross has applied some of his theories of international law which he has ably expounded in his Textbook of International Law.

The influence which the Charter of the United Nations is exercising on the development of world law is now manifest, and the powerful influence of the Organization in the maintenance of international peace is becoming more evident day by day. With the completion of the fourth year of United Nations activity it may be said that the Charter has furnished an adequate framework for the functioning of the Organization. The Charter is proving itself a living instrument under which increasingly complex and varied activities in the international sphere are being inaugurated and carried forward.

I take pleasure in commending Professor Ross' study of the Charter of the United Nations as an interesting, independent and scholarly analysis of this most important subject.

Trygve Lie.

CONTENTS

PREFACE

The years which have passed since the United Nations came into being have seen the growth of a vast amount of specialized literature concerned with the multifarious legal, political, or social problems connected with the new organization, its structure, functions, and practical activities, whereas — strangely enough — general expositions on the basis of a juridical analysis of the Charter are rare. Apart from *Leland M. Goodrich and Edvard Hambro*'s useful commentary there are, as far as I know, as yet no other works of this type than *Lazare Kopelmanas*' L'organisation des Nations Unies I (Paris 1947). And even of this very comprehensively planned work so far only the First Part of the First Volume comprising the legal sources of the United Nations is available.

Under these circumstances it is my hope that the present book may prove useful. Its aim is to give a general outline of the structure and functions of the organization. At the same time it has been kept within such moderate limits that it should be possible for the reader speedily to form a general idea of the problems. I have further tried to faciliate matters by distinguishing between main lines and details in the typographical arrangement.

It is self-evident that the exposition does not in any way claim to be exhaustive. Apart from the fact that the juridical imagination can never rise to the wealth of reality, and that practical experience is as yet rather limited, it has not been my intention to ferret out and absorb myself in all conceivable kinds of questions of interpretation, but only to create that general familiarity with the subject which is the necessary background to every reliable interpretation.

A special difficulty in the case of a book of this kind is the requirement that it should be topical. It is not possible to meet the desire that it should be up to date. The course of developments is rapid and does not stop while the author writes and the manuscript is translated, set in type, and printed. The sources are not available on the same day the incidents have taken place. Hence it has only been possible to include occasional references to events that have happened after the beginning of the year 1949. The revised edition of *Goodrich and Hambro*'s commentary has come to my hands so late that I could not weigh its additional information and views, although I have managed to adjust the references in my work made to the first edition of the commentary.

The translation, which has not been without difficulties, has been done by Miss Annie I. Fausbøll M. A. to whom I owe thanks for her careful and conscientious work.

Copenhagen, July 1949.

Alf Ross.

Introduction

THE ORIGIN AND GROWTH OF THE UNITED NATIONS

The Background.

When 50 nations signed the Charter of the United Nations at San Francisco on June, 26 1945, this attempt to establish a world organization for the maintenance of peace was not the first that had been made in the history of the world. Twice before there had been similar attempts after large-scale, devastating wars had come to an end. While the United Nations Charter was being signed the *League of Nations,* established after the first World War by the Treaty of Versailles of 1919, was still officially in existence. With the modifications necessitated by the experience of the intervening years, the League has largely served as a model for the organizational structure of the United Nations. In one respect, however, the United Nations is more like the *Holy Alliance* formed in Paris in 1815 by the sovereign monarchs of Austria, Prussia, and Russia, and subsequently adhered to not only by England and France, the two remaining great powers, but also by virtually all the other European states. Like the United Nations, the Holy Alliance was based, particularly at first, on the idea that the maintenance of peace must rest on agreement among the great powers and the collective use of their armed forces.

The notion of a peace organization can be traced much farther back than these attempts, although is was probably unknown in antiquity. The absolute supremacy of the Roman Empire over all other polities with which it came into contact was not good soil for the growth of an organization composed of powers of equal status. The Roman world peace was a *pax romana,* a peace based on the overriding power of a single state.

In the Middle Ages it was the menace of the Turks and the idea of the solidarity of all Christian nations which gave rise to the projects of leagues and organizations for fighting the common enemy and for the joint maintenance of peace. The earliest of these projects was put forward by the Frenchman *Pierre Dubois* who in 1306 published his *De recuperatione terrae sanctae.* Its fundamental idea was that peace among the Catholic princes was absolutely essential if the Holy Land was to be conquered. Hence a common council should be established, and quarrels between the princes should be referred to a court of arbitration having three lay and three ecclesiastical judges from whom appeals could be made to the pope. After the fall of Constantinople (1453) *Georg Podiebrad,* the King of Bohemia, put forward a similar proposal.

The best known project from the time that follows is the *Grand Dessein,* which was ascribed to *Henry IV* of France but whose author was actually the duke *de Sully* (c. 1635). According to this Europe was to be divided into 15 states which were to join in an alliance having a supreme council of 40 members nominated by the princes, the major states electing four, the smaller states less representatives.

In the 18th century, the age of rationalism, we find an abundance of schemes whose authors, unhampered by historical, social, and psychological considerations, thought it possible, by the light of reason and the law of nature, to lay down eternal principles for the maintenance of peace. Among these we find a publication entitled: *Abrégé du Projet de paix perpétuelle inventé par le roi Henri IV . . . approprié à l'état présent des affaires générales de Europe, démontré infiniment avantageux pour tous les hommes nés et a naitre ...* (1717) by the *Abbé de St. Pierre* (who had acted as secretary in the peace negotations at Utrecht in 1712). The great philosophers also devised projects, thus *Rousseau, Bentham,* and *Kant,* whose *Entwurf zum ewigen Frieden* marks the culmination and the end of this movement.

In the 19th century these abstract speculations died away, but at the same time a new, more realistic but less pretentious movement got started. The famous *Jay Treaty,* concluded in 1794 between the U.S.A. and the mother country, stipulated that various points of difference still remaining after the secession should be decided by arbitration. This inaugurated the modern movement in favour of arbitration, and paved the way for the two Hague Conferences of 1899 and 1907, by which the Permanent Court of Arbitration was established at the Hague and a number of treaties were concluded concerning war, neutrality, and pacific settlement of disputes. A third conference had been scheduled for the year 1915, and if the first world war had not occurred, it would undoubtedly have been possible by a continuation of these Hague conferences to find a way of establishing an international peace organization. Now this line of development was cut off. But, on the other hand, the first world war gave birth to the League of Nations.

The League of Nations and its Lesson.

The idea must already have been in the air. *Schücking-Wehberg*[1]) enumerates no less than 42 private drafts or schemes from the period 1914—19, mostly drawn up by various peace associations. It was of more importance that the suggestion rapidly gained adherents among statesmen. It was first put forward in France (Briand) and soon found

---

[1]) *Schücking-Wehberg,* Die Satzung des Völkerbundes (1921) 8.

favour in England. But the most important fact was that Mr. Wilson, the American president, sponsored the idea in what became a series of famous speeches. At the peace conference he insisted that the new covenant should be made "an integral part of the peace", the first chapter in the peace treaties. The League of Nations owed its existence in the first place to President Wilson, and it was felt as a strange irony of fate that the Senate should refuse to ratify the covenant. The U.S.A. never became a member of the League of Nations.

We do not of course propose to record the history of the League of Nations here. But it may not be without interest — as a background to the origin and problems of UN — briefly to recount its story. The League lived for two decades. The first of these was not without promise. The League actually succeeded in settling various disputes. In 1926 Germany joined and in 1925 the Locarno treaties for the stabilisation of peace in western Europe were negotiated. By the Briand-Kellogg Pact, concluded in Paris in 1928 and subscribed to by 58 states, recourse to war was solemnly condemned and the participants renounced war as an instrument of national policy in their relations with one other. During these years a certain optimism prevailed, associated with the names of Briand — Stresemann — Austen Chamberlain.

But in the thirties the League was faced with a number of conflicts which it could neither settle nor control. Lack of agreement among the members and reluctance to back up their statements by force of arms revealed the helplessness of the organization and entirely broke down its authority, so that at the outbreak of World War in 1939, it was deemed useless to call upon it. This decade saw the Japanese, Italian, and German aggressions, which merely provoked talk or half-measures. It started with Japan's onslaught on China (1931) and the conquest of Manchuria, which were only met by protests. Sanctions were, however, decided upon when Italy assailed Abyssinia (1935), but they were never seriously carried out. Italy could without difficulty have been brought to her knees merely by economic sanctions (an oil embargo), but the private interests of the great powers, their mutual fear and jealousy, rendered a firm policy impossible. Hitler too was given free rein in 1935 when he unilaterally cancelled the disarmament clauses of the Treaty of Versailles for Germany, and the following year occupied the demilitarized zone in the Rhineland. In the last years of the decade there followed fresh Japanese attacks on China, Italy's seizure of Albania, and the German invasion of Austria and Czechoslovakia (1938—39).

Why was the League of Nations politically a fiasco? A multitude of answers may no doubt be given to this question. I will merely, with Professor Brierly,[2]) point to a single elementary cause. The League was never based on that solidarity between the seven great powers then existant which alone could have guaranteed its success. The U.S. always remained outside. The U.S.S.R. could never regard the League as anything but an instrument for its own national policy. According to the Marxist philosophy universal peace can never be won through any form of organization in a capitalist world, but only after capitalism has been abolished in all countries. Again, there were the three aggressors (Japan, Italy, Germany) who obviously were ill-suited to play the part of guarantors of peace. Practically speaking then, only England and France were left, and we should not be far wrong in calling the League an Anglo-French Club. It is not to be wondered at that the burden became too heavy and that for these two countries too, the League gradually became an instrument for the furthering of their national policies.

---

2) *J. L. Brierly,* The Covenant and the Charter (1947) 6.

One thing emerges from the bitter lesson of these years. Solemn promises and pacts are not enough. The "Geneva idealism" of the twenties had a flavour of insincerity. More promises were made than were ever intended to be kept. There was an inflation of words and treaties. Men forgot that the world cannot be changed by a mere idealistic resolution. Marx scoffed at Utopian socialism which disregarded the laws governing social changes. In the same sense we may talk of an Utopian peace movement. If men wish to attain some social object they must be prepared to introduce the social conditions necessary for its achievement, for no one can arbitrarily interfere with the social machinery, without regard to the connection between cause and effect.

In a somewhat schematic form three possibilities may be conceived for the achievement of a universal peace. The first is based on force, a single state having made itself master of the world and founding a world-wide empire. This is peace after the pattern of the *pax romana*. The second is based on an idealistic belief in good-will and the sanctity of promises. This is the model of the Briand-Kellogg Pact. The third is based on that combination of force and moral obligation which is called law. The patterns here are the League and UN. The general idea is that it should be possible, in the relations between states, to monopolize violence and divert it into lawful channels so that it becomes a power for the maintenance of peace, just as individual states have succeeded in doing in their internal affairs. From an organization of states is evolved a federal state, a universal state.

Of these three possibilities the purely idealistic one must, as already stated, be regarded as a delusion, an Utopian misconception of the laws governing the working of human societies.

Hence, the only question that remains is whether peace is to be attained by violence or by law, i. e. by subjection to dictatorships or by democratic co-operation and the lawfully organized and monopolized exercise of force. The League of Nations and the United Nations are experiments in the latter alternative. We must sincerely hope that the UN will be successful. It is beyond doubt that the way before us is long and beset with untold difficulties. The integration of men in societies governed by law as known so far in history has been a very slow process. At the same time the latest technical innovations have for the first time in history made technically possible an empire comprising all the world. In the event of a third world war the result will probably be a dictatorship: a world empire — either American or Russian.

The Preparatory Work.

When during the second world war statesmen began to turn their attention to the organization of the peace after the war should have ceased, they might have been expected to harbour plans for some kind of reconstruction of the League. However, no one seems to have entertained this idea. The explanation is probably psychological. A great many unpleasant memories were associated with the League, the most recent being the exclusion of Russia owing to its assault on Finland. It seemed better to make a clean sweep and start all over again. This, indeed, appears from a number of solemn joint declarations on the problem of a peace organization which all refer to such an organization as a new departure and do not mention the League at all.

The first intimation is found in the Roosevelt-Churchill *Atlantic Charter* of August 14, 1941. The Charter was subscribed to and ratified by the Joint Declaration by the United Nations of January 1, 1942, signed by 26 nations including the USSR. In article 8 of the Atlantic Charter mention is made of "the establishment of a wider and permanent system of general security" as a future aim. In the *Moscow Declaration* of October 30, 1943, the four allied great powers recognized the necessity of establishing, at the earliest practicable date, a general international organization, based on the principle of the sovereign equality of all peace-loving states. At the *Yalta Conference* in February, 1945 it was possible to fix the time and place of a general conference for the drafting of a charter. It was decided that it should be called at San Francisco on April 25, 1945.

These solemn declarations were important because of their effect on public opinion. At the same time they established some of the principles on which the future organization was to be based, e. g. the self-determination of peoples, the sovereign equality of the states, and the universality of the organization.[3])

In the meantime a great deal of work had been done towards the drafting of the Charter. Once more the initiative was taken by the USA. An "advisory commission" under the leadership of Mr. *Cordell Hull,* Secretary of State, had been working on the question ever since the USA had entered the war. As a result of this work the American government, in Juli 1944, submitted a draft which was dispatched to the British, Chinese, and Soviet governments. Shortly afterwards each of these countries sent their own draft proposals to the American government, and the four drafts became the subject of close confidential talks at a meeting in *Dumbarton Oaks* near Washington from August 21 to October 7, 1944.[4])

---

3) Churchill and Roosevelt were originally in favour of a plurality of regional organizations but the American Secretary of State, Cordell Hull, fought with success for an over-all world organization, *Cordell Hull,* Memoirs (1948) Ch. 117.

4) *Cordell Hull* in his Memoirs (1948) 1625 f.f. gives a very instructive account of the preparatory work from the beginning and up to the San Francisco Conference.

A draft was agreed upon which was then made public. The main lines to be followed by the UN were here laid down. The subsequent conference in *San Francisco* made no essential changes in it. At Dumbarton Oaks, however, various questions of considerable political importance were left open, on which agreement could not be reached outstanding among these being the voting procedure in the Security Council and the principles for the administration of non-self-governing territories.[5]) Further, the question as to whether the Permanent Court of International Justice should be continued or a new international court should be established was deferred for the consideration of experts.

The political problems left open were settled at the *Yalta Conference* in February 1945 when agreement was reached concerning the voting procedure now to be found in Article 27 of the Charter, and the principles of the Trusteeship System were laid down. The question of the Permanent Court was decided in favour of a new court by a special committee of jurists meeting in Washington April, 9—20 1945.

There now only remained the convening of the general conference at San Francisco. It was summoned on April 25, 1945 for the final shaping and signing of the Charter.

The San Francisco Conference on International Organization (UNCIO) April 25 — June 26, 1948.

The sponsors were the four great powers which had drafted the Dumbarton Oaks proposals. Invitations were issued to 42 states, namely all such states as had signed or acceded to the Joint Declaration by the United Nations of January 1, 1942 and also declared war on Germany or

---

5) Others were the questions of initial membership and the liquidation of the League of Nations, see *Hull*, l. c., 1706.

Japan. The Conference further agreed to invite Argentina, the Byelorussian SSR (White Russia), the Ukrainian SSR (Ukraine), and Denmark. The Conference thus finally came to include a total of 50 states. The delegations (including advisers, technical experts and assistants of various kinds) of the individual states varied in number from 3 or 4 to the 175 members of the US. Altogether the conference comprised 282 delegates and 1,444 deputy delegates, advisers, technical experts, etc. besides the secretariat. In addition representatives of a number of international governmental agencies were invited.

The negotiations were organized as follows. Besides four general committees which were especially to deal with the central administration and coordination, four commissions were set up each with its own sphere and under each of these again a number of technical committees, 12 in all. Some of these appointed special subcommittees.

In deference to world public opinion the meetings took place in the full light of publicity. Only the discussions in the technical committees were closed, diplomatic experience having shown that this often facilitates the making of concessions and the arrival at agreement.[6])

The basis of the discussions was the Dumbarton Oaks proposals supplemented by the Yalta formula concerning the voting procedure in the Security Council and by various comments and proposed amendments submitted by the delegations to the Conference. Decisions on questions of procedure were made by simple majority, on other questions by a two-thirds majority of the votes cast.[7]) One vote was accorded to each state and the great powers had no privileges in this respect. At this point it should be kept in mind that the decisions had to do with the drafting of the Charter while the binding agreement only followed from subsequent

6) See further *Kopelmanas*, L'Organisation des Nations Unies (1947) 43 f.

7) See further *Kopelmanas*, l. c. 47 f.

ratification. In this way the great powers, whose ratification must be a *conditio sine qua non* could in point of fact retain a decisive influence independent of all rules of voting.

This was indeed what happened. It is true that there was no lack of criticism. Forty delegations proposed amendments, some 1200 in all. And on points of small importance the great powers did not oppose these amendments; they even seem to have encouraged them in order to strengthen the impression that the Charter was not to be a mere dictate on their part. But on really important issues the invited powers did not have their way with their criticisms or their amendments. A prolonged and detailed debate ensued, especially on the voting procedure dealt with in Article 27, which is actually the political cornerstone of the whole Charter. For some time the Conference seemed likely to go aground on this rock. There can hardly be any doubt that a free vote would have secured more than the necessary two-thirds majority for the various proposals advanced for the modification of the right of veto. But on this question the great powers would make no concessions. Dr. *Evatt,* the Australian delegate, who was the chief critic on this point, says that the great powers at last stated flatly that no change in the text would be accepted, and that the delegates would have to take the Charter with this text or have no world organization at all.[8])

The attempts of the invited powers to pass constructive amendments were further hampered by external circumstances. While the great powers appointed an unofficial inner committee for the settlement of mutual differences, the invited nations were divided, having no rallying point, and presenting no united front. Jealousy and a national predilection for their own schemes reduced their chances of favourable results.[9])

8) *Evatt,* The United Nations (1948) 24.

9) *Evatt,* l. c. 15; *Kopelmanas,* l. c. 80—82.

Below we enumerate the principal points on which the Dumbarton Oaks proposals were altered at San Francisco.[10])

(1) To the rules laid down for the action of the organization with regard to the pacific settlement of disputes was added a reference to the principles of justice and international law to prevent the rights of small states from being sacrificed to an appeasement policy after the manner of Munich.

(2) The powers of the General Assembly were extended to comprise the discussion of any question or any matter within the scope of the Charter. Subsequent experience has confirmed the great importance of this amendment.

(3) Criteria were laid down for the election of non-permanent members of the Security Council.

(4) Important concessions were made with regard to regional arrangements within the scope of the Charter, especially by the recognition of the right to collective self-defence (Article 51).

(5) The powers of the Economic and Social Council were extended, and the Council raised to the rank of a "principal organ."

(6) Finally, rules concerning the administration of non-self-governing territories, especially concerning the trusteeship system, were introduced.

The final result of the San Francisco conference was embodied in two treaties, both signed on June 26, 1945. One of these was the Charter of the United Nations consisting of 111 articles with the appended statute of the International Court comprising 70 articles. The other treaty has been called "Interim Arrangements". It comprises nine points dealing with the establishment of a Preparatory Commission for the performance of certain functions and arrangements for the first sessions of the General Assembly and the various councils, the establishment of the Secretariat, and the convening of the International Court of Justice.

In accordance with general practice the Charter had to be ratified in order to be binding on the signatories and to come into force. The rules for this were specified in Article 110. In accordance with these the Charter came into force

---

10) *Evatt,* l. c. 16 f.

on October 24, 1945. The organization came into being when the first session of the General Assembly was opened in London on January 10, 1946.

The minutes of the negotiations at San Francisco have been published in 15 volumes with an index, some 12,000 pages in all.[11] This preparatory work is not merely of historical interest but may provide important contributions towards the interpretation of doubtful cases by shedding light on the meaning and scope of the text as intended by the authors of the Charter. Of course equal weight cannot be attached to all pronouncements or resolutions in that respect. This is decided by the extent to which a pronouncement or resolution can be regarded as representative of a general or prevailing opinion. The greatest significance must be attached to the interpretative resolutions explanatory or supplementary to the text which the Conference passed unanimously in plenary session. Reports passed by committees, commissions or the Conference in plenary session will also frequently contain passages which can clarify the intentions of the authors. At this point, however, it should be kept in mind that the wording of the reports is usually the result of a compromise, and to understand the interests and attitudes involved it may be necessary to study the primary negotiations. Altogether it must be emphasized that the use of the preparatory documents for purposes of interpretation requires great tact and insight.

In my opinion there can be no doubt that in so far as the preparatory documents, as pointed out above, can be used as a means of interpretation, this interpretation must also be binding for such members of the organization as were not represented at the conference (Poland and admitted members).[12]

The Dissolution of the League of Nations.

After the creation of the UN there could be no doubt that the League must cease to exist. The matter could not, however, be arranged merely by its agreeing to its own dissolution. Various questions would need to be settled first, namely:

---

[11]) United Nations Conference on International Organization, San Francisco 1945: Documents. New York.

[12]) Cf. *Kopelmanas,* l. c. 307.

(1) The liquidation of the financial obligations of the League, especially to its staff.
(2) The transfer of certain material assets of the League to the United Nations, i. e. various buildings with their libraries, equipment etc.
(3) The transfer to the United Nations of various functions and powers exercised by the League either under the Covenant or special international agreements.

The first of these matters could be settled unilaterally by the League. It was done by resolutions adopted at the 21st and last session of the Assembly at Geneva from April 8 to 18, 1946 for the establishment of a Pensions Fund and a Board of Liquidation.[13])

The second question was solved by agreement between the two organizations, the assets in question being transferred to the United Nations on favourable terms. The sum to be transferred was not made payable in cash but the shares due to the various members of the UN were credited to them respectively in the books of the United Nations.[14])

The last question was settled by various resolutions adopted at the General Assembly of the UN, providing that all the functions of the League of a non-political character were to be carried on without breach of continuity by the UN or the specialized agencies connected with the UN.

(a) Functions and powers exercised by the League under *special international agreements.* The UN could not of course "appropriate" these by a unilateral resolution. The only point to be decided was whether the organization would agree to the transference of these functions by the contracting parties. By the resolution of the General Assembly of February 12, 1946 it was decided that[15])

— as regards functions of a *political* character, the organization would itself examine any request from the parties that the United Nations should assume the exercise of such functions;

---

13) See *The League Hands Over.* League of Nations (1946) 89 f.

14) L. c. 80—82; *Yearbook* 1946—47, 111.

15) *Yearbook* 1946—47, 110.

— as regards functions of a *technical and non-political* character, the United Nations was in principle willing to assume these. It was expressly added that the members, in so far as they were parties to the international agreement in question, by adopting the resolution should be considered as having assented to the transfer, and as having declared themselves willing to use their good offices to secure the co-operation of the other parties, so far as this should prove necessary.

(b) Functions exercised by the League on *its own initiative in accordance with the Covenant of the League.* — In the nature of the case only non-political functions come into question here. As soon as the commissions of the Economic and Social Council, the Secretariat, and the specialized agencies of the UN had been fully developed, it must be assumed that all non-political functions exercised by the League would have been transferred in so far as it was deemed desirable. The only object would then be to provide for continuity in the interim. By a resolution of December 14, 1946[16]) the Secretariat and the Economic and Social Council were authorized and requested to assume the non-political functions that had previously been performed by the Secretariat and various Commissions and Committees of the League, with the exception of functions entrusted to the specialized agencies.

The formal dissolution of the League was effected by the resolution of the Assembly of April 18, 1946, according to which the League of Nations, with effect from the following day, should cease to exist except for the sole purpose of liquidating its affairs. One item of the liquidation was the continuation of the non-political activities of the League until these could be assumed by UN or the specialized agencies connected with UN.

The lines I propose to follow in the remaining part of my exposition are these:

Part I will deal with some formal problems connected with the character of the Charter as the legal foundation of the United Nations. The Charter came into existence as a treaty, but it differs from most other treaties in the fact that it not only imposes various duties on the signatory

---

16) L. c., 263.

states but at the same time and primarily, — in common with national constitutions — sets up various organs empowered to act on behalf of the organization. The exposition will then fall naturally into two parts. One part will be concerned with the organizational structure of the United Nations, describing the composition and manner of functioning of the various organs (part II); the other part will deal with the functions of the organization as exercised by the various organs in connection with the obligations of the individual members as such (part III).

Finally the conclusion will sum up the characteristics of the organisation in its legal aspect.

It should be noted that Part I and the conclusion, being of a very theoretical nature, can without prejudice to the rest of the book be skipped by readers who lack the necessary knowledge of law or are not interested in these problems.

Part I

THE CHARTER AS THE LEGAL FOUNDATION OF THE UNITED NATIONS

The Formal Validity of the Charter.

In Article 110 (1 and 2) of the Charter it is laid down that the Charter is to be ratified and the ratifications are to be deposited with the Government of the United States of America. This agrees with the general international rule concerning the conclusion of international agreements, according to which a binding agreement as a rule is not brought about merely by the text being signed by the authorized negotiators. For the time being, the treaty is only a draft. It does not come into force until each of the contracting states has subscribed to the draft through their competent organs in a so-called declaration of ratification and has notified the other signatories. Each state can freely choose whether or not it will ratify the Charter. If, as stated above, it is said that the Charter *shall* be ratified, this cannot be understood to mean that it is a duty imposed on the parties; it only expresses the general rule that the legally binding validity of the Charter is dependent on ratification.

In Article 110 (3) it is further stated that the Charter is to come into force upon the deposit of the ratifications by the five great powers, and by the majority of the other signatory states. This condition had been complied with by October 24, 1945 and that day therefore is regarded as the birthday of the United Nations. The expression "come into force" is not really quite exact, in so far as it covers two different legal functions. Obviously what was meant was primarily that from the moment indicated, the Charter should be regarded as officially concluded between the states concerned. The Charter will then, as one sometimes says, have the *formal force of law,* i. e. from this moment the parties can no longer unilaterally release themselves from the contents and obligations of the Charter. Another question is from what moment the Charter requires the parties to fulfil their obligations. From that moment the agreement is said to have the *material force of law.* It will easily be understood that the two terms may not coincide. An agreement may have been validly concluded on January 1 so that the parties can no longer withdraw from it, though according to its own contents it may not require conforming behaviour until February 1. It is the latter of these two functions that is generally kept in view when a law or a treaty is said to "come into force".[1] The failure of the Charter to distinguish at this point between official "coming into existence" and "coming into force" indicates that the expression "come into force" is intended to cover them both, i. e. the treaty is to come into force (be conformed to according to its contents) from the moment it has been officially concluded.

It may be asked when the rules mentioned in Article 110 have obtained binding force. This question cannot be logically answered by a reference to the contents of these rules themselves. For then the validity of those rules would be taken for granted whose validity we set out to prove. The explanation must be that Article 110 is not an integral part of the Charter but a *special agreement* which became valid as soon as the Charter was signed on June 26, 1945 by virtue of the general international rule that the authorized negotiators may without ratification conclude binding agreements about the detailed conditions for the valid coming into existence and coming into force of the main agreement.[2]

The ratification requirement is stated more precisely in Article 110 (1) which lays down that ratification by the signatory states must be "*in accordance with their respective constitutional processes.*" This gives an answer to the question, much disputed in the theory of international law, whether a ratification has binding force if made in conflict with the constitutional rules of the state concerned, e. g. if the prescribed consent to the ratification has not been obtained from the legislative assembly. The question is settled to the effect that the ratification shall only be valid if these rules have been duly observed.[3]

---

1) As regards statutes the case is complicated by the fact that the "conforming behaviour" referred to may be either the application by the courts or the conforming behaviour of the citizens.

2) Cf. *Ross,* International Law, 215.

3) *Kopelmanas,* L'organisation, I 108—13, is of the opinion that the passage in question in Article 110 (1) also requires that the signatory power should have taken the necessary legislative measures for the internal execution of the pact as a condition of the validity of the ratification. He refers to the fact that ratification has increas-

There can hardly be any doubt that it must come within the competence of the authorized negotiators to register a protest for the state they represent in the special agreement.

The rules for the "coming into force" specified in paragraphs 3 and 4 must then be interpreted as follows. Only ratifications complying with the conditions stated in the first paragraph can be included in counting the number which is necessary before the Charter can come into force according to paragraph 3, and which under paragraph 4 make the states depositing their ratifications after that time original members of the organization; cf. Article 3 which, as a condition of original membership, requires ratification "in accordance with Article 110." The further requirement in paragraph 3, that *thereupon* the government of the United States of America shall draw up a protocol of the ratifications deposited, must mean that it is the duty of that government to see that the deposited ratifications really meet the requirement mentioned in paragraph 1, i. e. have been given in accordance with the special constitutional processes of the respective states.[4]

This however, was not done. The ratifications were simply accepted as they were. This has given rise to a defect in the formal validity of the Charter which may well be conceived to have unfortunate practical consequences. We may presumably disregard the possibility that the valid coming into existence of the organization itself will be disputed, whereas it cannot be excluded that a single state may subsequently deny its obligations on the plea that in giving its ratification it had violated constitutional rules. A similar plea has been put forward previously in the League of Nations.[5] Further it must be kept in mind that the ratifications were given at a time — the autumn of 1945 —

---

ingly acquired the effect of an automatic measure of execution. This interpretation must be emphatically rejected. The concept of ratification, according to theoretical as well as diplomatic usage, is clearly restricted to refer to the external declaration as a link in the conclusion of the treaty. Whether or not the ratification automatically involves internal execution (the latter is the case in not a few countries, amongst others Denmark) the ratification is one thing, the execution another which may be associated with the ratification as an effect. Has it ever been said that a state could not be held to have ratified a treaty, so long as it had not taken steps for its domestic implementation?

4) Kopelmanas holds the opposite view, l. c. 123.

5) On this view Luxembourg denied its obligation to join in sanctions against Italy, see *Kopelmanas,* l. c. 122 note 2.

when many constitutional systems throughout the world were in a more or less chaotic condition. One state even admitted that its ratification was not constitutionally in order, declaring at the same time that it intended to remedy the defect later on.[6])

Even though the legitimacy of a protest which might be conceived to arise out of a defective ratification could, according to the circumstances, be challenged from various juridical points of view, still the very possibility of a dispute must be termed a gross defect in the legal basis of the Charter which ought to be remedied as soon as possible. This might be done, as proposed by Kopelmanas,[7]) by a questionnaire from the UN to all the member states in which they were asked to state and confirm that the ratifications had taken place in accordance with their respective constitutional processes.

It must be regarded as a defect that Article 110 has given no time limit for the ratification of the signatures, nor regulated the right to ratify with reservations. Since, however, all the signatory powers had given ratifications without reservation before the end of the year 1945, this is of no practical importance.

A Treaty or a Constitution?

Is the Charter of the UN a treaty or a constitution — in the same sense as e. g. the constitution of the United States? The question is hardly of any practical importance; but since it is connected with fundamental concepts and theories of international law, it calls for a few remarks. The provisions of the Charter which it is important to consider are Article 2 (6) and Articles 108 and 109. References to them in the following are printed in ordinary type. The rest is of more theoretical interest.

The answer to this question naturally depends entirely on how we define the two concepts: treaty — legislative act (constitution). These terms, however, have not acquired so unambiguous a sense in scholarly usage that only one definition can be discussed. Without unduly straining current usage we can at any rate distinguish between two different definitions of these concepts.

---

[6]) The South African Union, see *Kopelmanas,* l. c. 122 note 2.

[7]) L. c. 125.

(1) In the first place we may emphasize the *basis of validity* implied in the *historical origin* of a certain institution, which therefore determines who will be subjects to this institution. On the one hand, a system of rules may be based on the *principle of the binding force of agreements* and so only bind the subjects who have given their consent to the introduction of the system. On the other hand, it may be based on the *principle of legislation,* i. e. some implied competence to give rules of law binding on other than those who have consented to the giving of them. In the former case, if the contracting parties are states, we have a treaty. In the latter we have legislation which, more precisely, is termed a constitution if it refers to the creation of an organization with appertaining legal competences.

This distinction is often made to signify that an order is international if it is based on treaty, constitutional if it based on legislation (constitution). This is the same as saying that international law is defined as law derived from agreements. As I have shown more fully in my Textbook of International Law (§ 1. V), such a definition is untenable, because it will exclude from international law large fields that must undoubtedly, according to the current view, be taken to belong to it.

That all international law in the current sense cannot be derived from agreement follows, if only from the fact that the fundamental norm itself, the rule that agreements must be kept — or rather the fundamental set of norms regulating the valid conclusion of treaties — cannot possibly, from a logical point of view, be based on agreement. To base the validity of agreements on an agreement to that effect is just as absurd as the answer given by a child who, being asked why it ought to obey its parents replies: because father and mother said so.

To this must be added the circumstance that international customary law cannot be regarded as based on consent, but is legislation in so far as it is binding on other states than those who have shared in the creation of the custom. If we hesitate to use the term legislation it is because we usually associate with this concept, besides the competence to bind others, the idea of resolutions passed by regular procedure.

If it has once been realized that international customs have the character of legislation it is not difficult to advance another step and see that the same may apply to that creation of law which is brought about in the form of treaties. The basic factor in custom, which conditions its force as "law", is the commonly (though not unanimously) held conception of law expressed in it.[8]) If now it can be similarly said about an arrangement which has come into being as a treaty that

---

8) *Ross,* Textbook of International Law, § 10 II.

on certain points it manifests a commonly held conception of law in the international community represented by the great majority of states (and is not therefore intended for the contracting parties alone) there is nothing strange in the fact that this pretention is regarded as legitimate and is actually able to take binding form. What happens here is not different from what happens in the creation of all customary law. In both cases the legal attitude rests on the fundamental norm for international legislation, that the manifest legal conviction, which is held by the great majority of states, is also binding for the remaining minority.

This consideration does not of course apply to bilateral treaties, or to collective treaties in general. The prerequisite must be the exceptional case that the treaty is concluded with the approval of the great majority of states in the world (or perhaps, especially in earlier times, within a certain region, e. g. Europe). Thus several European peace treaties in the 19th century purported to create a *droit public européen* binding on all European powers.[9]) The Hague Conventions of 1899 and 1907 have actually to a great extent had the effect of legislation binding on all states.

The Charter of the United Nations is of course *primarily a treaty* in the sense here indicated; historically it derives from the principle of the binding force of agreements and normally will only be binding on the contracting parties. But the above remarks will help us to see how it is possible that *on some points the Charter goes beyond this and shows the plain intention of legislation.* Since the Charter has been subscribed to by all the great powers and the great majority of states of any importance in the world, the pretention may in this case be said to be well founded. We can, however, only talk of an "intention" or a "pretention" as no ideology has as yet been established concerning the "power" to legislate in the form of treaties. Ultimately it will be a question of fact whether the intention can be carried through against the opposition of a third state; or whether it will be rejected as invalid and a transgression of the principle of the binding force of agreements. At this point we shall merely mention some instances in which the Charter undoubtedly shows the intention of legislating for third states.

Under *Article 2 (6)* the organization is to ensure "that states which are not members of the United Nations act in accordance with these principles so far as may be necessary for the maintenance of international peace and security".

---

[9]) *Ross*, l. c. § 10 I.

It may be open to some doubt what is included in the term "these principles". Presumably the principles referred to are those mentioned in the preceding paragraphs 3, 4, and 5, about the peaceful settlement of disputes, abstention from the use of force, and positive or negative assistance to the organization.[10] At any rate it is clear that this requires a certain conduct on the part of non-member states and that the organization is charged with enforcing behaviour conforming to these principles, if necessary, by enforcement action in accordance with Chapter VII.

During the negotiations in San Francisco the members fully recognized that legislative intention was present. It was defended by a reference to the fact that the purposes of the organization would be frustrated if outside states unopposed could commit acts of aggression or obstruct the organization's efforts to maintain peace, and that the United Nations, as *the most exalted expression of the international legal community,* must be entitled to act in such a way as to ensure effective co-operation from non-member states to the extent necessary for the maintenance of international peace and security.[11]

Legislative intention also occurs in *Article 103,* which provides that in the event of conflict between the obligations of the members of the United Nations under the Charter, and their obligations under any other international agreement, their obligations under the Charter shall prevail. "Any other international agreement" must fall into four groups:

(1) An agreement entered into between a member and *another member prior to* the acceptance of the Charter.

(2) An agreement entered into by a member and *another member after* acceptance of the Charter.

10) *A. Salomon,* Le préambule de la Charte, 180—85, thinks that only Article 2 (5) is referred to, but I do not find his arguments convincing.

11) UNCIO, VI, 354 f., 730, cited in *Salomon,* l. c. 183—84.

(3) An agreement entered into by a member and a *non-member prior to* the acceptance of the Charter.

(4) An agreement entered into by a member and a *non-member after* the acceptance of the Charter.

With reference to the problem here discussed — legislation for non-members — only groups 3 and 4 can come under consideration.

It is clear then that Article 103, so far as group 3 is concerned, lays down a rule which is in conflict with general international rules and which cannot be deduced from the principle of the binding force of agreements. If for instance a member prior to the Charter of the United Nations has concluded a pact of friendship and assistance or a commercial treaty with a non-member, and the organization subsequently imposes obligations on the member which are irreconcilable with this — e. g. in connection with economic or military measures of coercion directed either against the non-member in question (cf. Article 2 (6)) or against another state — it follows from generally accepted principles that the non-member's rights as based on the earlier agreement must take precedence over the claims of the organization. But Article 103 lays down the opposite rule. It deprives the non-member of acquired rights in favour of obligations under the Charter. This holds good even though Article 103 does not go so far as to declare the earlier agreement to be invalid. It merely lays down that the obligations under the Charter "shall prevail", that is to say, that non-members cannot demand specific performance of their treaty claims, though they can claim compensation for non-fulfilment.

As regards group 4 Article 103 does not provide anything but what follows from the general rules. A non-member that after accepting the Charter enters into an agreement with a member cannot thereby acquire rights prevailing over the obligations of the Charter.[12]

---

[12]) *Ross*, A Textbook of International Law, § 37, II.

(2) Once a certain institution has come into existence it is possible to consider it in the abstract, independently of its historical origin and the basis of validity implied by this. The institution may be regarded as a closed system which from the moment it has come validly into existence itself regulates the conditions governing valid resolutions for the amendment of the system and thus for the validity of the system as a whole. The concept of the *internal systematic basis of validity* differs from that of the historical basis of validity. It is defined by the rules of the system concerning its own *amendment.* If the unanimous consent of all the members is required, the basis of validity in an internal systematic sense is the principle of the binding force of agreements. If it can be amended in other ways it is the principle of legislation.

In accordance with this concept similar definitions may be given of the concepts of treaty versus legislation (constitution). Treaty is present when amendments require *unanimous assent,* legislation (constitution) when amendments can be made by *resolutions passed by a certain majority.* A famous example will illustrate the difference between the two concepts, taken respectively in their historical and their systematic sense. The American constitution of 1787/89 came into being in a historical sense as a treaty. It came into existence in accordance with the rules of amendment of the federation of 1777/81 by which ratification was required from all the 13 participating states.[13] After the new constitution had been passed by "The United States in Congress assembled", ratification, as is well known, took place in all the states, just as the Constitution itself in Article VII clearly implies that the new order is not binding on any state that has not ratified the document. On the other hand, the Constitution provides in Article V that future amendments may be made when ratified by three-fourths of the member states. In a systematic sense then it is a constitution, not a treaty.

This also applies to the Charter of the United Nations.

According to Article 108 amendments to the Charter are to come into force (i. e. be regarded as valid[14]) for all mem-

13) Article VII of the draft constitution however, departed from this principle, in so far as it was provided that ratification by 9 states should be sufficient for adoption by the ratifying states. Hence there was a will here to break up the federation but no deviation from the treaty principle. Further, for political reasons, provision was made for ratification by special conventions rather than by legislatures.

14) Cf. above p. 27—28.

bers when they have been adopted by two-thirds of the members[15]) of the General Assembly,[16]) and ratified in accordance with their respective constitutional processes by two-thirds of the members of the UN, including all the permanent members of the Security Council.

(This amendment procedure applies to all cases, even when amendments are adopted in a *general conference* called especially for this purpose, Article 109 (2). It is only with regard to the resolution to call such a general conference that Article 109 gives deviating rules. This resolution requires the same majority in the General Assembly and further a vote of any seven members of the Security Council (i. e., no veto); but no ratification is required. In a single instance, namely if such a conference has not been held before the 10th annual session of the General Assembly (1955), proposals for calling such a conference are to be placed on the agenda of that session and the conference is then to be held if so decided by a majority vote and by any seven members of the Security Council).

This means that *in a systematic respect the Charter is a constitution.* Its basis of validity is a competence to legislate exercised with respect to the members by the procedure indicated in Article 108.

---

15) This formulation viewed against the formulation in Article 18 suggests that the two-thirds are to be taken out of the total membership, not out of the number of voting members present. *Kopelmanas,* L'organisation, 152 note 1, adduces convincing arguments from the history of its evolution to show that this conclusion is unwarranted, and that the rules for voting in the General Assembly laid down in Article 108 as well as in Article 109 (1, 2, and 3) were intended to be identical with the arrangement according to Article 18.

16) Thus formally the great powers can exercise no veto against resolutions by the General Assembly, but actually this is of no importance as it would be futile to let a resolution pass on for ratification (subject to the veto) if one of the great powers had voted against the resolution in the General Assembly.

The question now arises as to the technical extent of this competence. It is specified in Article 108 as "amendments to the present Charter" which doubtless comprise not only amendments in a narrower sense but also additions to the Charter. It is worth noting that no reservation is made with regard to the fundamental provisions concerning the purpose of the Charter etc. Hence in a technical respect there can hardly be any limit to what may be regarded as an addition to the Charter; even provisions beyond or in conflict with the present purposes as defined in the Charter must be regarded as amendments or additions to these. The result will be that Article 108 introduces a *technically unlimited power* of legislation as regards the members.

These comments on the constitutional character of the Charter apply only to the wording of the Charter. Resolutions adopted in accordance with Article 108 are binding for all members as no right has been given of *withdrawing* from the organization. Actually, however, the legal position is largely modified by the declaration of interpretation incorporated in the report of Committee $I/_2$ and later approved both by Commission I and the Conference at San Francisco in plenary session. This report says that even though it is deemed the highest duty of the members to continue their co-operation, it is not the purpose of the organization, if a member feels constrained to withdraw because of exceptional circumstances, to compel that member to remain. Two such circumstances are exemplified. The rights and obligations of such members may have been changed by a Charter amendment in which the member in question does not concur; and an amendment adopted by the General Assembly (the implication being that the member in question has voted for it) may not have secured the necessary ratification.[17])

---

17) See *Leland M. Goodrich and Edvard Hambro,* Charter of the United Nations, Commentary and Documents, (1949, 2nd ed.), 143.

Hence though the declaration only states that coercion will not be brought to bear on a member wishing to withdraw it actually implies a recognition of the right to withdraw at one's own discretion.

This does not, however, entirely nullify the importance of the above-mentioned legislative power. Resolutions under Article 108 still bind states wishing to remain members of the UN. If the organization is permitted to develop in strength and universality, the pressure entailed by the disadvantage of a withdrawal may well become so great that the possibility of withdrawal will not mean any practical weakening of the effectivity of the legislative power — in the same way as e. g. the resolutions of the Universal Postal Union (UPU) are actually binding on all because no state can remain outside this partnership.

The rules for the amendment procedure were sharply criticized by the small states at the San Francisco Conference. The question was closely bound up with the disputed rules for voting in the Security Council, Article 27. Many of the delegates only reluctantly approved or failed to oppose the veto rule in Article 27 in the hope that it would be possible to alter this paragraph, at any rate later. Hence they were also bound to oppose the rules in Articles 108 and 109, which by establishing the right of the great powers to exercise the veto with regard to any amendment actually

— While the case first mentioned is in agreement with general treaty principles it must seem very strange that a state should be able to withdraw merely because an amendment is not adopted which was desired by a certain majority. The explanation of this remarkable provision is to be found only in the desire, expressed by many delegates, for a future amendment of Article 27. Hence the fulfilment of this wish has so to speak been accepted as a condition of remaining in the organization in so far as a right to withdraw has been conceded if this amendment is adopted with a two-thirds majority in the General Assembly but the necessary ratification is not obtained owing to the exercise of the veto.

renders the privileges of the great powers unassailable. Like Article 27, these paragraphs too were only carried after the great powers had unambiguously declared that failing this the Charter would not be ratified by them.[18])

The above-mentioned declaration of interpretation concerning permission to withdraw was made in order to meet the wishes of the opposition to some extent. But actually it must be supposed that it will only contribute to render revision still more difficult for fear that it would involve dissolution of the organization. For if a proposal for revision adopted by the General Assembly obtains the necessary ratification there is a risk that states which have not voted for the proposal will withdraw. And conversely, if the proposal is not ratified states which have voted for it may be expected to withdraw. The final result is a tendency only to pass proposals about which agreement can be reached.

The smaller states must especially deplore that the veto of the great powers can also be exercised in relation to alterations adopted at the General Conference which may be called at the 10th session. Some great Powers may disappear, new ones arise. The actual political constellations of power cannot be held in rein. The Charter affords no possibility of taking this into consideration. It reckons now and eternally with the present five great powers and no others. History has many examples of the desire to consolidate the *status quo* after a great war and give the peace conditions eternal validity. So far these attempts have all been frustrated by the dynamics of development. The Charter of the United Nations is another example of this tendency, and its fate is hardly likely to differ from that of its predecessors.

From a technical point of view it must be regarded as a defect that Articles 108 and 109 do not contain rules con-

---

18) See further *Kopelmanas*, L'organisation, 139 note 192.

cerning a time limit for ratification and the right of ratification with reservation.

From the preceding part it will appear that the adequate counterpart to the concept "treaty" (as the law relating to the binding force of agreements) is the concept "legislation" (legal rules binding others than those who have consented to them). The reason I have used the word "constitution" is partly that this is the traditional term under which the problem has usually been treated, and partly that the term "constitution" is generally used to designate an act of a fundamental content. If, as I consider appropriate, the term "constitution" is defined as having such content it does not conflict with the term "treaty". Whether an order is a "treaty" or a "legislative act", all according to its basis of validity, it must be called a "constitution" according to its content if it aims at creating organs for a collectivity and establishing corresponding powers. In this sense there can be no doubt that the Charter of the United Nations is a constitution — besides containing norms directly regulating the rights and duties of the members.

Part II

THE ORGANIZATIONAL STRUCTURE OF THE UNITED NATIONS

Chapter 1

MEMBERSHIP

Since the principal organs of the United Nations (Article 7), with the exception of the International Court of Justice and the Secretariat, consist either of all the members (the General Assembly) or of a certain more precisely defined group of these, the first step in a description of the organizational structure must be an account of the rules governing membership of the organization.

Principles.

An organization such as the UN, whose purpose is to ensure international peace and security, must naturally aim at *universality.* On the other hand, it may be argued that only such states should be admitted as fulfil certain *minimum requirements,* so that it cannot at the outset be assumed that they will either not be able or not be willing to meet the obligations imposed by the Charter and will therefore become a burden rather than an asset to the organization. It is the conflict between these two points of view which has determined the rules of the Charter concerning membership.

At the conference in San Francisco there were those who attached such importance to the desire for universality that they advocated compulsory membership for all states or at any rate proposed that membership in the organization should be open without conditions to any state desiring admission. These views did not, however, gain sufficient adherents. The result was that in principle the organization remains open insofar as any state has a right to claim admission though only if it, in the judgment of the organization, fulfills certain *elementary conditions.*

The Charter distinguishes between original and admitted members, but apart from the conditions of admission no legal effects attach to this. All who have once become members, no matter in what way, have the same rights and obligations under the Charter.

According to Article 3 the original members are the signatory powers which ratified the Charter in accordance with Article 110[2]), that is to say, the following 51 states:[3])

Argentine Republic	El Salvador	Norway
Australia	Ethiopia	Panama
Belgium	France	Paraguay
Bolivia	Greece	Peru
Brazil	Guatemala	Philippine Republic
Byelorussian SSR	Haiti	Poland
Canada	Honduras	Saudi Arabia
Chile	India	Syria
China	Iran	Turkey
Colombia	Iraq	Ukrainian SSR
Costa Rica	Lebanon	Union of South Africa
Cuba	Liberia	USSR
Czechoslovakia	Luxembourg	United Kingdom
Denmark	Mexico	United States
Dominican Republic	Netherlands	Uruguay
Ecuador	New Zealand	Venezuela
Egypt	Nicaragua	Yugoslavia

1) *Yearbook,* 1946—47, 20.

2) That is to say, in accordance with their constitutional processes, cf. above p. 28.

3) I. e. the 50 states at the San Francisco Conference and Poland which merely because its government was not at the time recog-

Under Article 4 membership is open to all peace-loving states which accept the obligations contained in the Charter and, in the judgment of the organization, are able and willing to carry out these obligations.

This implies the following four requirements.

(1) The applicant must be a *state.* The Charter gives no definition of what we should understand by this term. Doubts may be conceived to arise on two points.

In the first place as regards the degree *of "independence" or "sovereignty"* — more precisely described by the term "*self-government*" as defined in my Textbook of International Law, § 1, III — required for the community under consideration to be regarded as a state. That communities with merely municipal self-administration cannot be included must be taken for granted. A certain degree of self-government must undoubtedly be present. The only question is whether the community shall be fully self-governing, i. e. self-governing in all fields, or whether such communities should also be regarded as states which as member states of a federal state or as vassal states under a suzerain state, possess a more or less limited self-government. It would presumably be a natural requirement that there should be self-government in all the fields in which obligations may be incurred under the Charter, including especially the military field. In practice this would mean the exclusion of members of federal states and vassal states. This interpretation is hardly possible, however, seeing that among the original members (quite evidently regarded as states) there are two member states with, indeed, strictly limited self-government (White Russia and Ukraine). Under these circumstances there will be a wide latitude when the organization is to decide whether or not the legal status of an applicant is that of a state.

---

nized by all the sponsoring powers was not invited. When such recognition had taken place, Poland was invited to sign. The somewhat artificial formulation of Article 3 was chosen to cover Poland without mentioning it by name.

Secondly, where new nations are concerned the well known question will arise as to whether they have consolidated themselves in such a way that the conditions essential to their *recognition* as states are present. This point too must be settled by the organization at its own discretion. But the recognition by the organization that is implied in the admission is not binding on the members in the sense that it is equivalent to a recognition on the part of each individual member.

(2) The applicant must be *peace-loving*. It is self-evident that this expression is very vague and therefore leaves the way open to very free interpretation.

(3) The applicant is to *declare* that it will accept the obligations contained in the Charter. This requirement should hardly give rise to doubts.

(4) Finally the state must, in the judgment of the organization, *be able and willing to carry out these obligations*. As regards the objective requirement this must be subject to the qualification following from the fact that, as previously stated, states without full self-government are recognized as members. The requirement cannot mean that the constitutional conditions for carrying out the obligations of the Charter shall be present since a corresponding control was not exercised in the case of the original members. On this point too the decision must then depend on a very free interpretation on the part of the organization.

Under Article 4 (2) admission to membership is effected by a decision of the General Assembly on the recommendation of the Security Council[4]). In the General Assembly decisions concerning admission require a two-thirds majority (Article 18); in the Security Council the veto rule is applicable (Article 27).

---

4) Argentina on several occasions has argued that the recommendation of the Security Council called for in Article 4 need not necessarily mean a positive recommendation, but merely an expression of opinion on the part of the Council, see e. g. *Yearbook* 1947—48, 42.

The decision in each of the two bodies, according to the above comment on the nature of the conditions, is based on a very free interpretation. On the other hand, it must be maintained in view of the terms used in Article 4 ("membership is open to" ...., "the admission of any such state") that admission can only be refused if one or more of the four conditions enumerated are not complied with, and for no other reason. This was indeed established by the opinion given by the International Court of Justice on May 28, 1948 in the case relating to the *Conditions of admission of a State to membership in the United Nations.*[4a])

Practice.

At present eight states[5]) have been admitted to the UN, the number of members having thus risen to 59. On the other hand, a large number of states — at present 15 — have applied for membership without avail, the opposed political groups not having been able to reach agreement on the question in the Security Council. These are the following:

Albania	Portugal
Bulgaria	Trans-Jordan
Mongolian People's Republic	Austria
Rumania	Ceylon
Hungary	Nepal
Italy	Republic of Korea
Finland	People's Democratic Republic of Korea
Eire	

This politically motivated interpretation is clearly contrary to the Charter.

4a) Admission of a State to the United Nations (Charter, Art. 4), Advisory Opinion: I.C.T. Reports 1948, p. 57.

5) Afghanistan, Iceland, Sweden, Siam, Pakistan, Yemen, Burma and Israel.

As will be seen, these are chiefly states in political spheres of influence which one party suspects of being under the influence of the opposed party. On this point the political differences between the East and the West seem for the time being to have come to a deadlock. A number of the above-mentioned states have been applicants from as far back as 1946.

The conflict has also assumed a legal aspect as a dispute concerning the interpretation of Article 4 of the Charter. In a number of instances (Trans-Jordan, Eire, Portugal) Soviet Russia had exercised its veto, refusing membership on the ground that Russia did not maintain diplomatic relations with the applicant.[6]) Sometimes weight was also attached to the contribution of the states in question in the fight against Fascism.[7]) The opposing party maintained that it was in conflict with the Charter to base decisions on considerations not coming within the conditions of membership laid down in Article 4. The General Assembly then appealed, in a resolution of February 19, 1946[8]) to the Security Council to reconsider the applications refused "each according to its qualifications measured by the standards of the Charter and in accordance with Article 4". This resolution, however, made no difference in the attitude of the U.S.S.R. This power later voted down applications from Italy and Finland, not because it regarded these states as unsuited but because it would only consent to their admission if Albania, Bulgaria, and Rumania were simultaneously accepted as members. The General Assembly then passed a resolution on November 17, 1947 to solicit the opinion of the International Court of Justice partly as to whether it was justifiable to make consent to admission dependent on conditions not mentioned in Article 4, partly as to whether a member can make its vote for the admission of a state dependent on other states being admitted at the same time.[9]) In its advisory opinion of May 28, 1948 the Court answered both questions in the negative. The dispute thus ended in a victory for the view of the western powers. But this is of little practical importance. The opinion of the Court only means that Russia, if she would defer to the interpretation of the Court, will have to

---

6) Yearbook 1946—47, 417—18.

7) l. c. 124.

8) l. c. 125.

9) General Assembly, Official Records of the Second Session ..., Resolutions ..., Doc. A/519, p. 19.

give grounds for her opposition that accord with Article 4. In view of the very loose terms in which this article is couched that will not be difficult. Thus Ceylon's application (1948) was met by the objection that Ceylon did not possess the necessary independence and sovereignty as a state[10]) (though according to the amended constitution of February, 1948 Ceylon possesses the same independence as the other members of the British Commonwealth of Nations).

Establishment of Membership.

For the original members membership begins from the date of the deposit of their ratifications, the earliest date being October 24, 1945, Article 110 (3 and 4).

Membership for admitted members begins from the day the General Assembly votes for their admission.

Termination of Membership.

The Charter gives no rules for the discontinuance of membership by *withdrawal,* i. e. by a unilateral declaration to that effect on the part of a member. It is, however, actually made possible through the declaration of interpretation passed at the San Francisco Conference.

Further, membership can be brought to an end by *expulsion,* i. e. by the unilateral decision to that effect of the organization. Under Article 6 it can only be done if a member has persistently violated the principles of the Charter. The decision is made by the General Assembly (by a two-thirds majority vote) on the recommendation of the Security Council (subject to the veto), that is to say, it cannot be conceived to apply to any of the permanent members of the Security Council.

Expulsion might also be conceivable by an amendment of the Charter under Article 108, which is not dependent on definite conditions. The procedure is somewhat troublesome, since it requires ratification, but

10) United Nations Bulletin, vol. V (September 1, 1948) 705.

may be conceived to be employed when it is desired to expel a state without branding it as a persistent violator of the Charter, and perhaps also in cases when a state itself wishes to discontinue its membership but hesitates to do so by unilateral withdrawal. An amendment of the Charter for which it votes itself will have the character of discontinuance by agreement.

Suspension of Membership.

Under Article 5 the exercise of the rights and privileges of membership may be suspended when preventive or enforcement action — i. e. action in accordance with Chapter VII of the Charter — has been taken against the member in question by the Security Council.

The effects of suspension only apply to the rights, not to the obligations of members. As far as rights and privileges are concerned the state must be treated as a non-member as long as the suspension lasts; this especially means that it cannot be represented in the various organs composed of the members. On the other hand, this does not affect persons of the nationality of the suspended state with regard to the exercise of functions for which they have been chosen on account of their personal qualifications, not as representatives of a state, as for instance judges in the International Court of Justice or functionaries of the Secretariat.[11]

Again, suspension of membership differs from discontinuance by the possibility of restoration to normal membership. Under Article 5 this may take place by a decision to that effect made solely by the Security Council.

Suspension is effected by the decision of the General Assembly (by a two-thirds majority vote) on the recommendation of the Security Council (subject to the veto).

---

11) Likewise members of the two standing committees of the General Assembly on budgetary questions and on contributions respectively are not affected. The position as a trustee is probably not affected either, since this is based on a special agreement, and the trustee state in addition probably need not be a member of UN.

Chapter 2

OUTLINE OF THE STRUCTURE OF THE ORGANIZATION

Centralization and Functional Subdivision.[1])

An international organization with world-wide purposes of the type of the UN might be conceived to be organized in such a way that one organ alone attends to all the affairs of the organization. This organ might then for the technical preparation of a variety of matters appoint various committees in the same way as is done, for instance, in a legislative assembly. On this model uniformity and continuity in the conduct of the organization would be ensured. On the other hand, such a strict centralization would involve some disadvantages, which will be discussed below.

The opposite extreme would be present if a wide functional specialization of the tasks of the organization were carried out and these tasks were distributed among a number of autonomous mutually independent organs. Several advantages would undoubtedly result from this arrangement as counterparts to the disadvantages refered to above.

Thus there is reason to believe that the expert treatment of the various matters would be better if it were referred to organs composed with a view to that particular function. It is not merely that many of the delegates to a single central organ would lack the necessary specialized knowledge,

1) Cf. *Max Sørensen*, Some Observations on the Functional Principle in International Organization, *Jus Gentium* I (1949) 104 with references.

now with regard to one now with regard to another matter. It is of more importance that within the specialized organs it would be easier to segregate special subjects from the general ideological and political antagonisms which will often prevail in a single central organ, primarily elected with a view to political representation.

It will also, in case of a functional subdivision, be possible to vary appropriately the constitutional structure and voting procedure of the various organs so that influence and responsibility can be adjusted to the nature of the task and the interests at stake. While it will thus for instance be reasonable to secure to the great powers a decisive influence in the organ intended to undertake the political functions for the settlement of disputes and the maintenance of peace, there would, on the other hand, be good reason to give states such as Norway and Greece, which have great interests at stake in this field, an influence in an organ for the superintendence of international shipping affairs, an influence which they could never claim in purely political questions. Similarly, in the management of an international bank the voting power might well be assigned according to the financial engagements of the states in that undertaking while in most other respects a similar rule would be sheer absurdity.

The disadvantages of this system are that uniformity and coherence are lost. There would be no guarantee that the different organs would work harmoniously together. As in all over-organization, there is a risk that one hand does not know what the other hand is doing, that one measure may directly counteract another, that there will be either an overlapping or a complete vacuum of competences, in short a lack of harmony in the performance of the functions to the prejudice of the result.

The structure of the United Nations is a compromise between these two extremes.

The guiding principle has been that of creating a supreme organ invested with powers in every matter coming within the field of activity of the organization while at the same time a number of special functions are assigned to specialized organs, which, however, are subject to the instruction and supervision of the central organ. Sometimes the same pattern is repeated in several stages, the specialization being continued through sub-suborgans etc. Under this system the technical work will chiefly be carried out at the far ends of the ramification, i. e. by specialized organs with special powers. At the same time unity and coherence is ensured by the subordinate organs reporting to the superior organs, in the last instance to the central organ. The superior organs, more particularly the supreme organ, will then play a double rôle. They will act partly by giving instructions, supervising and co-ordinating the subordinate organs, partly by taking direct charge of all matters within their competence which have not been assigned to special hands.

The above-mentioned top, omnipotent organ of the UN is the *General Assembly* which according to Article 10 of the Charter

> "may discuss any questions or any matters within the scope of the present Charter or relating to the powers and functions of any organs provided for in the present Charter."

The specialized organs are the *Security Council,* the *Economic and Social Council,* the *Trusteeship Council,* and the *International Court of Justice.*

The guiding principle has not, however, been consistently carried through in all its purity.

In the first place the Security Council is not subject to the instruction and supervision of the General Assembly. Its purpose is to maintain international peace and security, i. e. it takes charge of the actual political functions, and exercises this function on its own authority. However, under Article 10, the General Assembly can, as already stated, discuss the powers and functions of the Council, i. e. it can express a criticism which need not be heeded. The independence of the Security Council does not mean, however, that political questions are withdrawn from the control of the General Assembly. On this point there is a curious double competence, the Security Council having the primary responsibility for the maintenance of peace and security (Article 24) and the power of the General Assembly being subject to that of the Security Council, according to certain rules (Article 12 (1) and Article 11 (2)) to be described in detail later on.

In the second place it is clear that the International Court of Justice is not subject to the instructions and supervision of the General Assembly. Further, it is hardly conceivable, even though Article 10 makes no reservation on this point, that the General Assembly would ever engage in a discussion of the powers and functions of the Court.

Also the Secretary-General to a great extent exercises a function on his own authority and the Secretariat accordingly is mentioned in Article 7 among the principal organs of the United Nations. At the same time the Secretariat also functions as a subsidiary organ to all the above-mentioned organs except the International Court.

Finally, the Charter implies that a considerable part of the tasks which come naturally within the scope of the organization's activities will be discharged by *autonomous international organizations*, which are not organs of the UN but have been established by special treaties. The Charter counts on this fact and takes for granted that the UN's own activities will for that reason be correspondingly curtailed. Further it provides that these agencies — as far as possible — shall be brought into relationship with the UN by the conclusion of agreements and that their activities shall be co-ordinated both mutually and with UN's own functions. If they have entered upon such agreements they are called *specialized agencies*. It is, however, clear that the specialized agencies are and will remain autonomous and so cannot be called organs of the UN. They are not subject to instruction and supervision, and the co-ordination aimed at does not afford the same guarantee of unity and harmony as would their position as subordinate organs under the UN.

We can then give the following outline of the structure of the organization in its main features:

Primary organs, i. e. such as are not subject to instruction and supervision by any other organ, are

The General Assembly
The Security Council
The International Court of Justice
The Seceraty-General.

Of these the General Assembly possesses the general comprehensive power, though with due deference to matters coming under the Court, and with the limitation flowing from the fact that its power in political affairs must to a certain extent yield to that of the Security Council.

Secondary organs under the General Assembly are

The Economic and Social Council
The Trusteeship Council[2]).

Brought into relation with the organization through the Economic and Social Council are

The Specialized Agencies.

A subsidiary organ to the other organs with the exception of the International Court is

The Secretariat.

The Specialized Agencies.

These are at present

A. *Agencies formed prior to and independently of the UN.*

1. *Universal Postal Union, UPU.*

Founded in 1874 at Bern, now comprising 88 na-

---

2) As regards the strategic trusteeship territories, the Trusteeship Council is subject to the Security Council, see below p. 96 and 182.

tions and territories, that is, practically the whole civilized world.

2. *International Labour Organization, ILO.*
   Founded in 1919 as an autonomous agency in connection with the League of Nations. The original members of ILO were identical with the original members of the League and membership in the League involved membership in ILO but was not a necessary condition. Several of the states that withdrew from the League remained members of ILO, while certain other states, e. g. the U.S.A., became members of ILO without entering the League. After a revision of its constitution 1945/46 the organization was in 1946 brought into relation with UN.
3. *International Telecommunication Union, ITU.*
   Founded at Madrid in 1932 as a successor to the International Telegraph Union of 1865.
4. *World Meteorological Organization, WMO.*
   Founded by a convention of October, 1947 as a successor to the International Meteorological Organization of 1878. WMO will come into being when the convention has been ratified by 30 states.

B. *Agencies founded prior to the UN but closely co-operating with the United Nations during the second world war.*

5. *Food and Agriculture Organization of the United Nations, FAO.*
   Projected at the UN Conference on Food and Agriculture at Hot Springs, Virginia, in May, 1943, it came into being in October, 1945.
6. *International Bank for Reconstruction and Development, BANK.*
   Founded at the Monetary and Financial Conference of the United Nations at Bretton Woods in July, 1944, it came into being in December, 1945.

7. *International Monetary Fund, FUND.*
Founded on the same occasion, it likewise came into being in December, 1945.
8. *International Civil Aviation Organization, ICAO.*
Founded at the conference in Chicago in November-December, 1944, it came into being in April, 1947.
9. *United Nations Educational, Scientific, and Cultural Organization, UNESCO.*
Founded at a conference in London in November, 1945, convened in accordance with proposals to that effect put forward at the San Francisco Conference, it came into being in November, 1946.

C. *Agencies founded at the instigation of the UN.*

10. *International Refugee Organization, IRO.*
Founded by a draft constitution prepared at the instance of the Economic and Social Council, approved by the General Assembly in December, 1946, and afterwards submitted for signing and ratification, IRO came into being in August, 1948.
11. *World Health Organization, WHO.*
Founded at the International Health Conference called by the Economic and Social Council in New York in June-July, 1946, it came into being in April, 1948.
12. *International Trade Organization, ITO.*
Founded at the UN Conference on Trade and Employment convened in November, 1947 — March, 1948, at the instigation of the Economic and Social Council. The ITO will come into being when the Havana Charter has been ratified by the required number of signatory states.
13. *Intergovernmental Maritime Consultative Organization, IMCO.*

Founded at the UN Maritime Conference in Geneva in February-March 1948, convened at the instance of the Economic and Social Council, IMCO will come formally into existence when twenty-one states have become parties to the Convention, of which seven must each have a total tonnage of at least one million gross tons of shipping.

Chapter 3

THE GENERAL ASSEMBLY

In a certain sense the General Assembly may be regarded as the highest organ of the United Nations. That does not mean that all other organs — certainly not the Security Council and the International Court — derive their authority from the Assembly and are subject to its instruction and supervision. But under Article 10 the General Assembly possesses the highest moral authority in so far as it can discuss (and thus criticize) the competence and functions of any other organ — even though it must be assumed that this authority will scarcely be exercised in relation to the Court. Further, in a technical respect the competence of the Assembly comprises every subject coming within the scope of the Charter, though with due regard for matters coming under the Court, and limited by the fact that in political questions the competence of the General Assembly must sometimes yield to that of the Security Council.

It is futile to draw parallels with current parliamentary constitutional organs and to compare the General Assembly to the parliament of a democratic state. The circumstances are too dissimilar. In particular, the General Assembly has no legislative power nor the power to decide on the composition of a government,[1] the two functions primarily characterizing a parliament.

On the other hand, the General Assembly may in so far be termed a World Parliament as it is the highest forum for

1) According to the socalled parliamentary system, not accepted in the United States.

the discussion and criticism of all matters within the scope of the United Nations; in short, the highest organ of world public opinion. It is the place where the immediate problems of the world political situation are debated, and its composition is a guarantee that each state has the opportunity to raise its voice and be heard by the whole world. It is a matter of course that this chance to appeal to the United Nations gathered in the General Assembly, and thus to the public conscience of the world, is a moral guarantee which may serve to prevent injustices and smooth out conflicts. On the other hand, we must not be blind to the fact that, as indeed experience has shown, the very appeal to world public opinion may make the Assembly an instrument of extensive political propaganda, with the delegates speaking over each other's heads, actuated more by the propagandistic effect of their speeches than by the wish to solve a conflict, so that the real work for a solution must largely take place behind the scenes.

Composition.

Under Article 9 the General Assembly is to consist of all members of the United Nations, each member having at most five representatives. It should be noted that according to this the "members" of the General Assembly are the states, not the representatives; cf. Article 18, under which each member, i. e. each state, no matter what is the number of its representatives, has one vote. The reason why a member may have up to five representatives is the purely technical one that it would not be possible for a single person to manage the work in the various committees and subcommittees into which the Assembly has organized itself.

Under rule 21 of the Rules of Procedure, the range of representation has been extended, for in addition to the five representatives each delegation may further consist of five alternate representatives and as many advisers, experts, and persons of similar status as may be desired. An alternate may take the place of a representative and the other members of a delegation may be elected as members of committees. They cannot, however, be presidents, vice-presidents, or rapporteurs on these, unless they are given the status of alternates.[1a)]

Scope and Nature of Powers.

Postponing the detailed discussion of the functions of the United Nations to a later section, we shall here briefly outline the scope and character of the competences assigned to the various organs.

The powers of the General Assembly, as far as the exercise of the functions relating to the United Nations' specialized *technical purposes* are concerned, are dealt with in articles 10—16. Of these Article 10 contains the general rule that the Assembly may discuss any question or any matter within the scope of the Charter and — except as provided in Article 12 — may make recommendations to the members as well as to the Security Council, or to both on any such question or matter. The remaining articles do not limit the scope of this provision. Their purport is either to emphasize particularly important examples of it or to impose the duty of initiative on the General Assembly.

From Articles 11, 12, 13(1a), 14, and 15 it appears that the General Assembly also has express power to deal with political matters for which the Security Council has the chief responsibility. Its competence in the economic and social field is mentioned in Articles 13, 14, and 16, which partly refer to the detailed rules in Chapters IX—XII including the exercise of functions that take place through the Economic and Social Council and the Trusteeship Council respectively.

Further the General Assembly has a number of *organizational-technical* powers mentioned in various parts of the Charter. These refer especially to decisions concerning membership, election of members of various organs, co-operation

1a) General Assembly, Rules of Procedure, Rules 22 and 92.

in amendments of the Charter, authority in the financial matters of the organization, and instruction and supervision of secondary organs.

Thus the General Assembly exercises constituent functions with regard to membership of the organization (admission, expulsion, suspension; Articles 4—6); to the election of members for various organs (the non-permanent members of the Security Council, Article 23 (2); the Economic and Social Council, Article 61; some of the members of the Trusteeship Council, Article 86 (1c), and the members of the International Court of Justice, Articles 4, 8, 10, 12 of the Statute of the Court; and to the appointment of the Secretary-General, Article 97.

Under Articles 108 and 109 the co-operation of the General Assembly is required for amendments to the Charter, and under Article 17 it has power of controlling the financial matters of the organization, since it considers and approves the budget and allocates the expenses to be borne by the members.

Finally the General Assembly has instructive and supervisory powers in relation to the organs subordinate to it, Articles 15, 60, 85; and power to approve agreements with specialized agencies and trusteeship agreements, Articles 63 and 85.

While the decisions of the General Assembly in these latter technical matters of the organization are legally binding (either for the members or for the organ in question), its authority for the promotion of the specialized purposes of the organization can never, according to Articles 10—16, assume a higher degree of authority than that of a recommendation. The Assembly can *never legislate, never order or command, but only submit, recommend, propose.* Even though the line between these stages, legally, is absolute and sharp, the practical difference in international relations will often be relative and fluid. On the one hand, the binding force of the legal obligations in this field is unfortunately in many cases not strictly maintained, while on the other hand a "recommendation" issuing from an organ such as the General Assembly of UN will frequently — especially if the great powers have agreed upon it — have a moral and political motivating force which makes it more effective than many a legal norm. Hence there is no reason to attach too much weight to the fact that the Assembly can never go beyond the mild mode of recommendation. If the United Nations are successful enough to develop harmoniously and establish their authority, this form will not prevent the General Assembly from acting according to the motto "*suaviter in modo, fortiter in re.*"

Within the merely "advisory" power of the Assembly three phases can be distinguished. They are
(1) *Investigation,* i. e. an activity aiming solely at ascertaining facts and their relationship. The purpose may be the negative one of dispelling wrong and exaggerated notions which are a source of conflict; or the positive one of letting the facts speak for themselves. Article 10 does not expressly mention this phase which, however, must be supposed to be implied in the others. Formally the powers of the General Assembly may find expression in a decision that a certain investigation be carried out or in a decision as to what must, in the opinion of the Assembly, be regarded as established by a certain investigation.
(2) *Discussion,* i. e. a mutual exchange of views among the delegates for the interpretation of facts and the solution of problems. Its value lies primarily in the opportunity it gives the members to influence each other by well-documented arguments and negotiations over compromises. The competence to discuss matters must, however, also include the power to make decisions which either sum up the statements made or in which the Assembly as such sets forth its opinion, in so far as this has not the character of a recommendation.
(3) *Recommendation,* i. e. the legally non-binding invitation to act in a certain way.

Voting.

Each member of the General Assembly (i. e. each state) has one vote, Article 18 (1).

Decisions of the General Assembly on "important questions" are to be made by a two-thirds majority of the members present and voting, on other questions decisions are made by a simple majority.

"Important questions" include

(a) The questions enumerated in Article 18 (2), see the Charter;
(b) Amendments to the Charter and the convening of a general conference, Articles 108 and 109 (1 and 2);
(c) Additional categories of questions according to the decision of the General Assembly made by a majority vote of the members present and voting (Article 18 (3)).

Collectively these statements must be considered as exhaustive, so that no matter can at discretion be characterized as an "important question" if a majority resolution to that effect cannot be obtained in the Assembly.

The power to do so under Article 18 (3) — which can only refer to groups of questions, not to a single question as such — means that a simple majority waives the power it would otherwise have had as such to make a decision. Since, however, a resolution to that effect can be overruled by a later resolution of a simple majority in the opposite direction, the restriction the majority imposes on itself is not hard. The majority may at any time reassume its power.

It will appear from these rules for voting that the great powers have not been given privileges of any kind in the General Assembly, either as regards the number of votes they hold, or the passing of resolutions. The General Assembly is democratic in its procedure as well as its composition.

The rule that resolutions on important questions require a majority of two-thirds will, it may be conceived, tend to make decisions impossible because, in spite of attempts to find a suitable formulation, it may not prove possible to arrive at a standpoint which will attract the required majority. The possibility of a negative result may become fatal in matters, the positive settling of which is essential to the function of the organization, as e. g. the elections to the various organs mentioned in Article 18 (2). Already at the first elections to the Security Council and the Economic and Social Council despite repeated voting it was not possible to obtain the necessary two-thirds majority for the last state that was to be elected in order to obtain the full number. The difficulty was overcome in both cases by one of the competing states voluntarily yielding to another.[2] A similar situation occurred later at the re-election to the Economic and Social Council, and this time it was solved by a member which was not due to resign voluntarily giving up its seat.[3] Obviously, it is not reassuring that the constitution of the organization depends on the generosity of individual members.

Rules of Procedure.

The General Assembly — like the earlier parliaments — is not conceived of as a permanently functioning organ. Normally it is to meet in regular session once a year, commencing on the third Tuesday in September.[4] In addition it can, if special circumstances render it necessary, be summoned for special sessions by the Secretary-General on request of the Security Council or of a majority of the members of the United Nations.

Experience has shown that there may be a need for the General Assembly to deal with current political questions outside the annual sessions. Due partly to the differences that have developed between the groups of powers, the Security Council which acts under the pressure of the veto rule has been greatly hampered in its political efficiency, while the General Assembly, less constrained, has increasingly utilized its powers under the Charter to deal with political questions — though deferring to the prerogative of the Security Council. The more the Security Council has been paralyzed and unable to discharge with vigour and authority the main responsibility for the maintenance of international peace and security imposed on it by the Charter, the more the General Assembly has become the organ

---

2) In the elections for the Security Council Canada withdrew in favour of Australia, in the elections for the Economic and Social Council New Zealand withdrew in favour of Yugoslavia, *Yearbook* 1946—47, 60.

3) Belgium withdrew in order that both Holland and Turkey might be elected, *Yearbook* 1946—47, 118.

4) Article 20 and Rules of Procedure, Rule 1.

through which the United Nations has had to exercise its influence if the organization were not entirely to lose its prestige and authority. However, summoning of the General Assembly for special sessions is a large and troublesome undertaking. In view of this circumstance it was resolved at the second session of the General Assembly (November 1947), at the instance af the US, to appoint an *Interim Committee* (also called the "Little Assembly") composed of one representative of each member state, whose chief task was to be to deal with and report on political questions arising in the period between the second and third regular sessions which it was desired to place on the agenda of the General Assembly.[5]) The American proposal was severely criticized by the Soviet representative, who declared that it was an attempt to create a new organ not anticipated by the Charter for the undermining of the Security Council, and therefore a flagrant breach of the Charter. Referring to this declaration the Soviet Union, White Russia, Ukraine, Czechoslovakia, Poland, and Yugoslavia refused to take part in its work. There can hardly be any doubt, however, that the appointment of the Interim Committee is entirely lawful under Article 22 of the Charter which allows the General Assembly to establish such subsidiary organs as it considers necessary for the performance of its functions. Politically too, the idea seems right so long as it is not possible by an amendment to the veto rule to enable the Security Council to carry out its task in a satisfactory way and thus assert the authority of the United Nations. By a large majority the Assembly in its third session decided to re-establish its Interim Committee for the period up to the next regular session.

The General Assembly adopts its own rules of procedure.

---

5) Official Records of the Second Session General Assembly, Resolutions Doc. A/519, p. 15.

According to these all meetings of the Assembly itself, as well as of its main committees and other committees or subsidiary organs, are to be held in public, unless the organ concerned decides otherwise, which in the Assembly and its main committees can only take place under exceptional circumstances.[6]

Since the Assembly does not, like a parliament, consist of parties, the representation on committees is not proportional. No nomination of candidates takes place. The state or persons that obtain the number of votes required are considered to be elected.

When only one elective place is to be filled and a two-thirds majority is required for the election, the balloting is continued until one candidate has obtained the required number of votes. If the third ballot proves inconclusive, the voting alternates, according to certain rules, between ballots restricted to the two candidates that obtained the greatest number of votes and unrestricted ballots.

When several elective places are to be filled, those candidates are declared to be elected who have obtained the required majority after the first ballot. If the number of these is less than the number to be elected, the voting is continued, being now restricted to the candidates obtaining the greatest number of votes in the last ballot, to a number not more than twice the places remaining to be filled. If three such ballots are inconclusive, the voting alternates according to certain rules between restricted and unrestricted ballots.[7]

As already pointed out, these rules may make it impossible to effect an election.

Organization.

The General Assembly which, as we saw, includes up to five representatives for each member, — that is, at present up to 295 representatives — is naturally a slow-moving instrument. The effective preparation of the matters dealt with must take place in smaller bodies, committees, partly

6) Rules of Procedure, Rules 55 and 150.

7) Rules of Procedure, Rules 85 and 86.

composed with a view to the special qualifications of the members to deal with a certain group of affairs.

Not only representatives proper but also other members of the delegations may be appointed members of committees.[8]) The General Assembly may set up such committees as it deems necessary,[9]) but the rules of procedure provide that a number of regular committees shall be established.

These *ordinary committees* are:
(1) Six main committees whose task it is to prepare the subjects on the agenda of the Assembly and draft resolutions. Each delegation has the right to appoint one member to each of these committees. The subjects are distributed among them as follows:[10])

1. Political and Security matters
2. Economic and Financial matters
3. Social, Humanitarian and Cultural matters
4. Trusteeship matters
5. Administrative and Budgetary matters
6. Legal matters.

(2) The Credentials Committee consisting of nine members elected for each session, its task being to examine the credentials of the delegates.[11])
(3) The General Committe consisting of the president of the General Assembly its seven vice presidents, and the chairmen of the six main committees. It is to consider the provisional agenda, co-ordinate the committee work, and assist the president in the conduct of the work.[12])
(4) The Administrative and Budgetary Committee consisting of nine members elected for three years and on the basis of their personal qualifications.[13])
(5) The Committee on Contributions consisting of ten members elected in the same way.[14])

In addition the General Assembly can, as previously stated, establish such committees at it deems desirable. There may especially be a question of *ad hoc committees* for the treatment of individual tasks, such as the above-mentioned Interim Committee, the Provisional Commission on

---

[8]) See above, note 1.
[9]) Rules of Procedure, Rule 88.
[10]) Rules of Procedure, Rules 90—91.
[11]) Rules of Procedure, Rules 24—25.
[12]) Rules of Procedure, Rules 33—37.
[13]) Rules of Procedure, Rules 144—146.
[14]) Rules of Procedure, Rules 147—149.

Korea,[15] the special Balkan Committee, and the Headquarters Committee.

Under Article 22 the General Assembly can establish such ***subsidiary organs*** as it deems necessary for the performance of its function. As to whether or not a committee comes under the term "subsidiary organ", the language seems somewhat vague.[16] The decisive thing, however, is simply that this concept must be conceived of more broadly so that it will also apply to organs that do not, like committees, consist exclusively of delegates. As an example of special importance we may mention the *International Law Commission* composed of 15 eminent jurists chosen for their high qualitications in the field of international law and representing as a whole the chief forms of civilization and the basic legal systems of the world. The general object of the commission is the promotion of the progressive development of international law and its codification. At its 1st session (1949) the commission has tentatively selected 14 subjects for codification; priority was given to 3 topics: (1) law of treaties; (2) arbitral procedure, and (3) regime on the high seas. Within this general framework the commission has dealt with 3 specific items: (1) the drafting of a declaration on the rights and duties of states; (2) the formulation of the principles recognized in the Charter of the Nüremberg Tribunal and in the judgment of this Tribunal; and (3) the study of the desirability and possibility of establishing an international judicial organ for the trial of persons charged with genocide or other crimes over which jurisdiction will be conferred upon that organ by international conventions.[17] [18]

---

15) The fact that ad hoc committees are sometimes called commissions is probably accidental and without fundamental importance.

16) Thus e. g. Rule 150, cf. Rule 88, would seem to distinguish between committees and subsidiary organs, whereas the Interim Committee just mentioned calls itself a subsidiary organ.

17) See Statute of the International Law Commission, Resolution 174 (II), November 21, 1947; Report of the International Law Commission, 1. session, Off. Records G. A., 4. session Suppl. No. 10 (A/925).

18) The description given here of the organization of the General Assembly deviates from that given in the UN's own official expositions, see e. g. *Yearbook* (1946—47) 53 and *Everyman's United Nations* (1948) 9—10. According to these a distinction is made between four types of Committees:

(1) Main Committes	(2) Procedural Committees
(3) Standing Committees	(4) Ad hoc Committees.

This division is not based on any definite principle. What could be the basis for such a division?

Chapter 4

THE SECURITY COUNCIL

The Security Council may perhaps be said to be the police station of the United Nations. It has the main responsibility for the maintenance of peace and order, that is to say for peace and security, in the international community. True, it has not at its disposal its own forces to exercise this responsibility. The idea is that the Council, as the occasion requires, should order out the members to function as police. However, the detailed agreements implied by the Charter as a basis for this function, have not yet been negotiated. Until this happens, Article 106 refers to concerted action by the great powers on behalf of the organization for the maintenance of peace and security. Seeing that, under the present circumstances, there does not appear to be any great prospect of such concerted action, the United Nations are in fact for the present paralyzed in their exercise of power, and the Security Council must be content to act as best it can, using other means. Since, however, the highest moral authority lies with the General Assembly, and the power of action of the Security Council is further paralyzed by the disagreement of the great powers and the veto rule, it is understandable that the centre of gravity, even in political matters, has tended more and more to shift to the General Assembly.

As previously stated, the Council is one of the principal organs of the organization, i. e. it is not subject to instruction and supervision by the General Assembly, apart from the right of the latter to criticize as provided in Article 10.

Composition.

In order that the Security Council may function according to its purpose it is conceived as a small compact organ. Under Article 23 it consists of eleven members, each having only one representative. On the view that, in the nature of the case, it must usually be the great powers that bear the burden of acting as international custodians of order, these have been given a privileged seat on the Council. The five great powers are permanent members. The remaining six are elected by the General Assembly. In the election of these the factors to be taken into account are

(1) in the first instance the contributions of members of the United Nations to the maintenance of international peace and security and to the other purposes of the organization, and further

(2) equitable geographical distribution.

The latter factor makes it possible even for small states which have no power worth mention to join the council. The considerations coming into question, however, are stated to be "special", not exhaustive. Hence they merely indicate a non-binding norm.

The election is valid for a term of two years. No retiring member can be immediately re-elected. In this way the arrangement known from the League of Nations with semi-permanent membership for the benefit of certain states of middle size has been excluded, and the possibility of smaller states joining the council has been enhanced.

Scope and Nature of Powers.

The powers of the Security Council are restricted to political matters but comprise all such, not only coercive measures according to Chapter VII but also the pacific settlement of disputes according to Chapter VI.

The Council bears the primary responsibility for the

maintenance of international peace and security (Article 24). This is shown by the Council taking precedence over the General Assembly in this field. Under Article 12 (1) the latter cannot make any recommendation in a dispute or situation as long as the Security Council is exercising the functions assigned to it by the Charter in the matter in question. Further the Council alone can make binding decisions concerning enforcement action in accordance with Chapter VII. Hence every question that requires such action is to be referred to the Council by the General Assembly, Article 11 (2).[1)]

Depending on their contents the resolutions of the Council may have different degrees of authority. Resolutions under Chapter VI for the peaceful settlement of disputes can never pass beyond the stage of recommendation. On the other hand, under Chapter VII the Council can make decisions in a narrower sense, that is to say legally binding decisions, calling for members' participation in enforcement action in the event of a violation or of a threat to the peace. Under Article 25 the members have undertaken to recognize and carry out the resolutions of the Security Council in this narrower sense.[2)]

---

1) See further below, p. 153 f. The Council has also some organizational powers relating to membership (Articles 4—6), the designation of the Secretary-General (Article 97) and the election of members of the International Court (Article 4 of the Statute).

2) The use of the word "decision" in the Charter is very confusing. In the rules for voting in Articles 18, 27, 67, and 89 the term is obviously used as synonymous with any adoption of a measure, no matter what its contents, hence also about the adoption of recommendations. In Articles 40 and 94, on the other hand, the term is expressly contrasted with recommendations and must mean the legally binding adoption of a motion. The same sense seems implied in Articles 41, 44, 48, and 49. Finally in the statute of the International Court the term "decision" is used about various kinds of decisions, sometimes equivalent to judgment (Article 59), sometimes without any such sense (Article 16 and 17).

But in another sense all the decisions of the Council, recommendations as well as actual resolutions, are binding. Article 24 states that the members have conferred on the Security Council the primary responsibility for the maintenance of peace and security and that they are agreed that the Council in carrying out its duties under this responsibility acts on their behalf. While it may no doubt be said about any organ that it acts on behalf of the organization, it is here laid down that the Security Council acts on behalf of the individual members. This in connection with the above-mentioned responsibility conferred on the Council can only mean that the single members are bound by the decisions of the Council, having thus waived the right for instance to resist, politically, a recommendation by the Council for the settlement of a dispute or the like.

Voting.

The voting procedure of the Security Council was no doubt the point which gave rise to most criticism and conflict at the San Francisco Conference, and later to bitterness and disappointment. Attempts are still being made to modify the right of veto, and many are of the opinion that until a reform on this point is carried out there can be no prospect of the Security Council functioning so as to fulfill its obligations in the spirit of the Charter.

The Dumbarton Oaks proposals contained no rules on this point, because the four great powers could not agree upon a solution. It was only at the meeting at Yalta in February, 1945 that a formula was agreed upon which is now embodied without amendment in Article 27 of the Charter.

Under this article three different rules can be applied to the adoption of proposals.

The main rule, coming into operation if none of the deviations are indicated, is that for the adoption of a proposal the affirmative votes of seven members are required, including affirmative votes of all the permanent members *(absolute veto).*

Decisions on proposals concerning procedural matters require the affirmative votes of seven members *(no veto).*

Decisions on proposals under Chapter VI and Article 52 (3), i. e. cases concerning the peaceful settlement of disputes, require seven affirmative votes, including affirmative votes from all the permanent members of the council who are not parties to the dispute in question, while any member who is a party to the dispute must abstain from voting *(conditional veto).*

Hence in all cases a qualified majority of seven out of eleven votes is required. What varies is merely the right of veto. The majority requirement increases automatically in the last-mentioned situation, i. e. in decisions concerning pacific settlement. Since every member which is a party to the dispute is excluded from voting without the number of affirmative votes required being diminished, the seven votes will come to constitute an increasing percentage of the members eligible to vote, the more members are concerned in the dispute. This would seem to be technically indefensible. In cases in which five or more members are involved the result will be quite absurd, as the Security Council will then be incapable of passing resolutions.[3])

This aspect of Article 27 does not so far seem to have been noticed, perhaps due to the fact that interest has centred round the veto rules.

The idea behind this rule is that agreement between the great powers is the fundamental condition of organized cooperation for the maintenance of peace. In the present state

---

[3]) The situation is by no means inconceivable. In the dispute about the blockade of Berlin four of the members of the Council were thus implicated. This was presumably one of the reasons why the dispute was brought before the Council under Chapter VII.

of the world no great power can be expected to be willing to put its military machinery into operation in order to enforce a resolution for which it has not been able to vote.[4]) Any attempt to set the great machine going in circumstances when the great powers disagree may bring about the opposite result of that intended, may become the cause of war between the great powers instead of a step towards the maintenance of peace. These considerations, it is true, take us no farther than to acknowledge the veto in cases where action is required. But it is further protested, any resolution in a political question may entail consequences not to be envisaged and become the first link in a chain of events compelling the Security Council to set the enforcement machinery in operation.[5]) Hence the veto rule must be extended to apply to all political questions — if they are not of a purely procedural character.

I do not think it can be denied that this system in itself is based on a sound respect for facts, which differs in a salutary way from the voluble but unreal treaties of the Geneva idealism of the 20s. The only question is whether the veto has not been given too wide a scope.

The system has produced greater disadvantages than anticipated at any rate by the Western Powers. Of course from the very first it was clear to everybody that the price paid for the veto rule was that it precludes the use of the Charter against any great power. Even though many feel aggrieved that the latter will thus evade earthly justice, this concession to realism would no doubt be well grounded if political control of all the other powers could thereby be made the more effective.

But it is at this very point that we find the greatest weakness of the system. If the Charter is to funcion as intended

4) Cf. "Statement" of June 7, 1945, point 9, quoted in *Goodrich and Hambro*, 218.

5) L. c., point 4.

the assumption is that the five great powers are able to co-operate in harmony and unity. If this is not the case, if a deep chasm opens between the permanent members of the Council, the organization will have no teeth in it not only where great powers are concerned, but quite generally. And when the veto is extended to comprise any political question and not merely the use of the coercive apparatus, the Security Council will lose all power to assert its authority.

It must be remembered that Article 27, like the Yalta formula, came into being during the war under the influence of an optimistic belief that the agreement and co-operation which had proved possible during the struggle with the common foe could be continued in peace time as well. The Yalta declaration of February 11, 1945 concludes with the following characteristic statement:

> IX. *Unity for Peace as for War.* Our meeting here in the Crimea has reaffirmed our common determination to maintain and strengthen in the peace to come that unity of purpose and of action which has made victory possible and certain for the United Nations in this war. We believe that this is a sacred obligation which our governments owe to our peoples and to all the peoples of the world.
>
> Only with the continuing and growing cooperation and understanding among our three countries and among all the peace-loving nations can the highest aspiration of humanity be realized — a secure and lasting peace which will in the words of the Atlantic Charter, "afford assurance that all the men in all the lands may live out their lives in freedom from fear and want."
>
> Victory in this war and establishment of the proposed international organization will provide the greatest opportunity in all history to create in the years to come the essential conditions of such a peace.

Such was the talk in 1945. Later developments have proved them wrong. Thus the conditions for the far-reaching right of veto have broken down.

There has been no want of warning voices. At the San Francisco Conference violent objections were raised against the Yalta agreement in many quarters. Criticism, led by Dr.

Evatt, the Australian delegate, was directed especially against two points.

In the first place it was demanded that the veto should be limited to questions concerning enforcement action.[6]) It was asserted that the Council had a duty, not simply a right, to settle disputes, so that no member would have the right to oppose resolutions aimed solely at pacific settlement. An Australian amendment obtained 10 affirmative votes, 20 were against, and 15 abstained from voting, a result that must be ascribed to the clearly expressed standpoint of the great powers that the Charter would not be ratified if the Yalta formula were not accepted unconditionally.

---

6) It appears from *The Memoirs of Cordell Hull* (1948) 1652 cp. 1663 and 1683 that the original American draft required the concurring votes of all permanent members only on four categories of questions. "These were: the final terms of settlement of disputes; the regulation of armaments and armed forces; the determination of threats to the peace, of breaches of the peace, and of acts obstructing measures for the maintenance of security and peace; and the institution and application of measures of enforcement." It seems, according to Hull, as if the subsequent discussions with the Russians focused upon the question whether a party to a dispute could vote in his own case or not. President Roosevelt was indefatigable in stressing that a right to vote would be against all rules of civil justice and the principles imbedded by the forefathers in American law. Several personal messages on this question were delivered directly to Stalin. (l. c. 1677—78, 1680, 1683, 1700, 1705). At Dumbarton Oaks a compromise formula was worked out as a basis for discussion according to which a party was deprived from voting only so long as enforcement action was not involved. The voting formula agreed upon at Yalta is almost identical with this compromise formula. Cordell Hull, however, nowhere mentions any discussion with the Russians concerning the fundamental problem, what kind of decisions require the concurrent vote of all the permanent members. One gets the impression that the Anglo-American negotiators were sidetracked by the morally important, but politically comparatively insignificant question of the right to vote in one's own case and for this reason neglected or forgot the politically really important question of the province of the veto.

Second, clarification was demanded. On many points doubts arose as to the practical application of the formula, and it turned out that the great powers themselves disagreed about its interpretation. A list of 23 problems was drawn up with questions as to what would be the voting procedure in each of these under the Yalta formula. The great powers then consulted together and on June 7, 1945 issued a joint "statement" for the interpretation of the voting rules.[7]) This statement set forth general views but did not give the desired clarity, as it only answered one of the 23 questions directly. Further it voiced the optimistic view that it must be considered improbable that any question of great importance would arise in the future about which it might be doubtful whether or not the veto should be exercised.

This "statement" was never actually approved and adopted by the conference, hence formally its contribution to the interpretation is not legally binding. But it is obvious that the greatest weight must be attached to this declaration on which the major powers were agreed.

In answer to the repeatedly expressed anxiety that the veto rule might lead to abuse by obstructing the work of the Security Council the great powers here too gave frequent assurances that this fear was unfounded.

In face of this optimism and firmness on the part of the leading powers criticism had to yield. But later developments have proved in a most deplorable way that it was not groundless. The Security Council has become a battlefield of the policies of the great powers, and the veto right has been used as a weapon in this struggle.

A counting[8]) shows that, by the end of 1947, 165 votings had taken place in the Security Council on questions of substance, i. e. questions to which the veto rule in Article 27

---

7) Reprinted in *Goodrich and Hambro,* 216.

8) *Norman J. Padelford,* The Use of the Veto, *Intern. Org.* II (1948) 227 f., 231.

(3) can be applied. In 70 cases the required affirmative votes were not obtained. Among the remaining 95 cases the adoption of 23 was prevented by the exercise of the veto. In 21 of these cases the veto was exercised by Russia alone, in one case by Russia and France, and in one case by France alone.

Perhaps these statistics do not mean very much. It must be taken into account that the distribution of seats on the Council means that Russia must often resort to the veto to prevent a decision, while the western powers need only muster five votes to achieve the same result, by virtue of the majority rule.

The decisive thing is the way in which the veto has been exercised in a number of cases.

In the case concerning the presence of British and French troops in Syria and Lebanon (February, 1946) both these great powers declared themselves willing to withdraw their troops. The only disagreement referred to minor technical questions as to the time when and the rate at which it should be done. Under these circumstances the majority of the members desired a resolution in somewhat milder terms than that first proposed by Lebanon. Russia defeated this proposal by its veto — not because it did not desire the withdrawal of the troops, but because the resolution was not comprehensive enough. The result was that no resolution was passed at all. If England and France had not loyally declared that they were willing to consider themselves bound by the conditions laid down in the defeated proposal, the Council's treatment of the matter would have been quite ineffective.[9])

A similar outcome was seen in the question of the Spanish régime in April—June 1946. Poland here proposed that by joint action under Articles 39 and 41 the members should be enjoined to break off diplomatic relations with Spain. The majority held the opinion that the conditions for action under Chapter VII were not present and proposed the recommendation of interruption of diplomatic relations as a measure under Article 36. In this case too Russia exercised its veto, merely because it did not consider the resolution far-reaching enough.[10]) It is evident that none of the views put forward in favour of the veto right

9) *Yearbook* 1946—47, 341—45.

10) l. c. 345—51.

can render legitimate use like this, which is clearly only a political demonstration, without regard to the desire for agreement and at the expense of interests the vetoing member himself shared.

With respect to the admission of new members, too, the Russian veto has been vigorously exercised, in conflict with earlier promises,[11]) in conflict with the rules for admission in Article 4,[12]) and evidently for the purpose of preventing admission of states which might be supposed to strengthen the position of the western powers in UN.

Even outside the above-mentioned clear cases of abuse, the Russian veto has largely been exercised, not because Russia desired to oppose resolutions which might be supposed to entail consequences for Russia which that country did not wish to accept, but simply for the protection of Russian vassal states against measures taken by the organization for the maintenance of peace and security.[13])

The problems of interpretation to which Article 27 gives rise must in the first place be concerned with the cases forming exceptions to the use of the veto, i. e. "no veto" and "conditional veto".

(1) "No veto" comes into operation when the matter to be voted on is a *procedural matter.* When is this the case?

To enable us to formulate the rule in this way, without enumerating a list of the matters coming under that head, it should be possible to give the word "procedure" a clear, definite meaning according to general usage or scientific theory, setting it apart from the treatment of matters of substance and acceptable for the interpretation of Article 27. That, however, is not possible. The Charter itself in Article 36 (1 and 2) uses the word "procedure" in the sense of "course of action" for the settling of disputes (such as arbitration and the like), i. e. about measures which are

---

11) In the Potsdam Declaration of August 2, 1945 the Soviet Union declared itself willing to recommend the admission of Italy and Finland (in addition to Bulgaria, Hungary and Rumania) when a peace treaty had been concluded with these countries.

12) See above p. 43—45.

13) See *Padelford,* l. c., 227 f., 237.

clearly a part of the treatment of matters of substance. The question will then arise whether it is possible to draw a distinction between "procedure" in this wider sense and "procedure" in a certain narrower sense in which the word is used in Article 27 (2). This question must be answered in the negative, so far as resolutions with regard to a concrete case under consideration are concerned. All such resolutions, from the resolution to hear a party and to establish a commission of enquiry or the like, to the final settlement of the case, form one continuous chain in which every single link is a step towards the solution of matters of substance and is therefore at the same time both a "procedure" and a "treatment of matters of substance". To contrast these concepts in principle is absurd.

If there is to be any possibility at all of defining the term "procedure" and giving it a definitive meaning there is no recourse but to identify it with *the abstract rules concerning organizational technical matters,* usually called "rules of procedure". These include the rules concerning the selection of a president, the holding of meetings etc., rules as to whether an interested party may be invited to take part in a meeting (but not the concrete decision on this question), etc.

This definition, in principle the only conceivable one, cannot be used in the interpretation of Article 27. The result would be that the veto would only be excluded in questions of ordinary amendments of the procedure or in decisions concerning the latter, e. g. concerning the selection of a president, the appointment of a meeting place and the like, which are entirely unconnected with any concrete case. On the other hand, the veto could be exercised in the case of any resolution aiming at a concrete case. Such an interpretation of the term "procedure", I maintain, cannot be used to interpret Article 27, since it appears unambiguously from the negotiations in San Francisco, particularly from the "statement" issued by the great powers on June 7, 1945, that Article 27 (2) is to be applied — and the veto thus be excluded — also in connection with certain decisions that are items in the treatment of a concrete matter.[14]) Thus the "statement" has not accepted the only conceivable, really sharp criterion. It seems rather to have attached importance to the question whether the decision is directly concerned with or in its consequences may be conceived to entail enforcement action. But this view is quite vague and in many cases of no use whatever.

Hence the result is that in the interpretation of Article 27 (2) we entirely lack any principle from which to start, if we want to decide what matters are procedural and thus not subject to exercise of the veto. Without perhaps realizing it, and at any rate without admitting it, the great powers have in fact passed on to a *casual enumeration* — without drawing up the list of instances which in that case is necessary. Lacking the courage to make a decision they have shirked a delicate problem in the hope that matters would be sure to come out all right. But they did not come out all right. The definition of the right of veto has already caused many conflicts and is sure to give rise to more.[15])

---

14) Thus decisions on (1) inviting an interested state to participate in the discussion; (2) to consider or discuss a dispute or situation brought to the attention of the Council under article 35; (3) to hear the parties in such a dispute; and (4) to remind the Members of the Organization of their general obligations assumed under the Charter as regards the peaceful settlement of international disputes.

15) Doubts may especially arise in regard to preliminary questions concerning actual facts which condition the competence of the Council in certain respects. Thus e. g. the treatment of all matters of substance under Chapter VI is conditioned by the existence of a "dispute or situation likely to endanger the maintenance of international peace and security." Is the settling of the question as to whether or not this condition is fulfilled a matter of procedure or a matter of substance? The lack of clarity on this point and the fear of calling forth a Russian veto by pushing matters to extremes underlie the formal disagreements in the Iranian question. On the part of the

Now it is by no means unheard of, and as a rule it is no insurmountable disaster, that a legal rule is based on an unclear and challengeable concept. Through the authorita-

---

U.S.A. it was attempted to get round the difficulty by passing a resolution which, indeed, formally referred solely to the procedure and came within that right to "consider and discuss" which cannot be vetoed (cf. above note 14, point 2), but which by summing up the discussion could with some justice be said actually to be a camouflaged treatment of a matter of substance, see further *Clyde Eagleton,* The Jurisdiction of the Security Council over Disputes, 40, Am. Journ. 1946, 513 f. particularly 528—33 and below p. 105. — In a number of cases it is of importance whether or not a certain state is party to a dispute. Experience has shown that implicated powers are often decidedly reluctant to recognize the existence of a dispute but at most will admit that there is a "situation". Is the deciding of this important question a procedural matter or a matter of substance? In the Syrian-Lebanese case it was maintained by the Egyptian representative that the question was one of procedure, while the representative of the Soviet Union held the opposite view (*Yearbook* 1946—47, 341). — Doubts may also arise with respect to the estimation of the concrete contents of a resolution. It may be, for instance, that a resolution which is in the main concerned with a procedural matter is also thought to affect substantive issues. At the meeting of the Security Council on June 26, 1946 a resolution was passed on the Spanish question with nine votes against two (Russia and Poland). The president declared the resolution to have been carried. The Russian representative entered a protest against this, maintaining that the resolution was partly of a non-procedural character. This question was then put to the vote. There were eight affirmative against two negative votes (U.S.S.R. and France), with one abstention (Poland). After this the resolution must be regarded as defeated since the question as to whether or not a matter is procedural is itself subject to veto, cf. the text below p. 82. (*Yearbook,* 1946—47, 350). — According to the same method ("double veto") the Soviet Union in the 202nd meeting of the Security Council on September 15, 1947 prevented the passing of a resolution that a request (according to Article 12) to the General Assembly that the Assembly make a recommendation on a dispute or a situation in respect of which the Security Council is exercising the functions assigned to it in the Charter, is procedural. S. C. Off. Rec. 2. year 2390 f.

tive interpretation of the Courts, a guidance in the application of it will gradually grow up to remedy the defect.

The present case is otherwise. If there is a difference of opinion as to whether a matter comes into one or the other category the Council itself settles the dispute. But what is the voting procedure in that case? As to this point the "statement" lays down that this preliminary question is to be decided according to the veto rule in Article 27 (3), which must mean that the veto can be exercised against the decision to characterize the matter as a procedural question, with the effect that the ordinary primary rule of Article 27 (3) must be applied.[16])

Actually this means that the exception for procedural questions in Article 27 (2) in the more detailed decisions of the "statement" has only a morally binding force. *Formally any of the permanent members can legally, at any time and in any question under discussion, dispute its procedural character and then, in the ensuing voting, veto a resolution in which the procedural character of the matter is established. And after this the veto rule is applied to the matter in question.*[17])

(2) "*Conditional veto*" is used when the matter is concerned with the pacific settlement of a dispute. A member

---

16) This happened in the Spanish question, see note 15 at the end.

17) The representative of the U.S. in the Interim Committee says in his report of July 15, 1948 on the Voting in the Security Council (doc. A/578 *Intern. Org.* III (1949) 193) "that the San Francisco statement had been abused by the Union of Soviet Socialist Republics as regards the application of part II of that document. The Soviet Union had prevented the Security Council from declaring certain items procedural which, under the Charter, were clearly procedural. The San Francisco Statement was never intended to be used for such a purpose. The purpose of part II of the statement was to provide a method for determining how to settle the voting procedure applicable to additional categories of decisions not specifically designated as procedural or non-procedural."

then can only vote — and a permanent member only exercise the veto — on condition that it is not a party to the dispute. Even though this rule will in most cases hardly give rise to doubt in a *bona fide* application, it may nevertheless be eluded. The Charter throughout makes a distinction between a "dispute" and a "situation". If now the implicated permanent member holds that there is only a "situation", and that it has therefore a vote (veto), there is here a preliminary question which must be settled by the Council. It may be doubtful whether this preliminary question is a substantive or a procedural issue. But in any case this doubly preliminary question, according to the "statement", is decided under veto regarding its characterization as procedural. If then the first preliminary question as to whether or not there is a dispute is to be settled as a question of substance, the permanent member interested can exercise its veto with the result that it retains its right of voting (veto) in the primary question of a pacific settlement.[18])

Thus this exception to the main rule likewise has only morally binding force. *The net result with regard to Article 27 (2 and 3) is, then, that a major power which would disregard moral considerations can push through its veto against any resolution passed in the Security Council, without exception.*

(3) In connection with the application of the primary rule concerning absolute veto the question has arisen whether a resolution can be regarded as validly carried if one of the permanent members has abstained from voting. On a literal interpretation of Article 27 the question must be answered in the negative. Article 27, as we saw, requires seven affirmative votes including affirmative votes from all the perman-

18) In the above-mentioned report the Interim Committee has proposed a definition of the term "dispute" for the purposes of Article 27 (3), see *Intern. Org.* III (1949) 201, 196.

ent members. However, a permanent practice has now grown up according to which abstention from voting is not regarded as involving the exercise of the veto, but the resolution is considered valid despite the wording of Article 27.[19])

The criticism of Article 27 voiced at the San Francisco Conference has not died down since then. Experience has only given it more weight. Countless deliberations have taken place, and many proposals have been put forward in order to find a more acceptable solution.

Such proposals as aimed at a formal amendment of Article 27 of the Charter have not had any prospect of gaining adherents, in view of the existing rules governing amendments which also allow the right of veto against amendments to the Charter.

There would seem to be some chance of reaching an informal agreement between the permanent members of the Council concerning the rules for exercising the veto on the model indicated by the "Statement" of the great powers dated June 7, 1945.

Committee 1 of the General Assembly took up the question, at its very first session, while recently the Interim Committee has subjected the voting rules in the Security Council to very close investigation and analysis.

The Interim Committee's report[20]) is based on a list comprizing 98 possible questions on which the Security Council might be called upon to make decisions under the Charter or the Statute of the International

---

19) In the debate in the General Assembly (May 11, 1949) on the admission of Israel, Iraq objected to the Security Council's recommendation as being invalid on account of the abstention of the United Kingdom, a permanent member, in the vote. The President of the Assembly ruled that the recommendation must be accepted as a recommendation of the Council within the meaning of the Charter, *Bulletin* VI (1949) 556—57. Probably the same rule will apply also to the case of absence from meetings.

20) Reports of the Interim Committee of the General Assembly (5. Jan. to 5. Aug. 1948). The Problem of Voting in the Security Council, Doc. A/578, 15. July 1948 — Paris 1948.

Court. On the basis thereof the Committee proposed that the General Assembly should

(1) Recommend to the members of the Security Council that they deem 36 items enumerated in the list of possible decisions of the Security Council to be procedural and conduct their business accordingly.

(2) Recommend to the permanent members of the Security Council that they agree that another 21 items on the list should be adopted by the vote of any seven members, whether the decisions are considered procedural or non-procedural.

The items indicated include among others:

— Recommendations for the admission of a state to membership.
— The question as to whether or not a decision is procedural under the voting rule of Article 27 (2).
— Whether a question is a situation or a dispute under the voting rule of Article 27 (3).
— All decisions concerning a pacific settlement under Chapter VI, in so far as they have not already been designated as procedural.

(3) Recommend to the permanent members of the Security Council that they agree among themselves to consult with one another before a vote is taken, especially if their unanimity is required to enable the Security Council to function effectively; and further to agree that they will only exercise the veto when the question is of vital importance and at any rate never because a proposal does not go far enough to satisfy them.

(4) Recommend to the members of the United Nations that in agreements conferring functions on the Security Council such conditions of voting within this body be provided as would exclude the application of the rule of unanimity of the permanent members.

After being dealt with in the political *ad hoc* committee of the General Assembly, a resolution in accordance with these proposals was passed by 43 votes against 6, with 2 abstentions, in the second part of the third session of the General Assembly in New York in 1949. It should be kept in mind, however, that we are here concerned with various recommendations only, and that these will hardly lead to any result unless all the permanent members of the Security Council are willing to accept them. The attitude of the U.S.S.R. in this respect will appear from the draft resolution it submitted on the same occasion, in which the unanimity principle is mentioned as the most important condition for ensuring effective action by the organization for the maintenance of peace, and in which it expresses confidence that in the future the Security Council will seek to improve the possibility of adopting concerted decisions by applying the method of consultation where necessary.

Rules of Procedure.

Under Article 28 the Security Council — as appropriate to a police station — is to be so organized as to be able to function continuously. Each member of the Council shall for this purpose be represented at all times at the seat of the organization. The word "continuously" is not, however, quite correct. Naturally there is not to be an unbroken watch night and day. It simply means "at any time".[21])

Periodic meetings are held twice a year at times fixed by the Council. The president may summon a meeting at any time he deems necessary, but the intervals between the meetings must not exceed fourteen days. Further, he shall call a meeting at the request of any member of the Council, and in some other cases.[22])

The presidency of the Security Council is held in turn for one month at a time by the members in the English alphabetical order of their names.[23])

States which are not members of the Council, even such as are not members of the organization, can, if their interests are specially affected, be invited to participate in the meetings of the Council, without vote, according to the rules specified in Articles 31 and 32.

Organization.

Owing to the small number of members that go to compose the Security Council, and to its limited sphere of activity, the setting up of committees among its members is not of the same importance as in the General Assembly. The rules of procedure only establish one *ordinary committee*, namely for the admission of new members.[24])

It is of greater importance that the Council may set up

---

21) It may also be interpreted to mean that the Security Council is in continuous session, i. e. can be called at any time.

22) Rules of Procedure, 1—4.

23) R. of Pr. 18.

24) R. of Pr. 59.

committees (commissions)[25]) for the discussion of special questions *(ad hoc)* or set up *subsidiary organs* whose composition is not limited to representatives of the members of the Council.[26])

At its first meeting the Council appointed a committee for the purpose of revising the rules of procedure (the committee of experts).[27])

As other examples of *ad hoc* committees may be mentioned the Commission for the Regulation of Armed Forces, the Balkan Commission, the Indonesian Committee, the Kashmir Commission etc.

The Atomic Energy Commission was established by the General Assembly but comes under the Security Council and must be regarded as a subsidiary organ, since besides the members of the Council it also includes Canada.

Article 47 (cf. Article 26) lays down that a Military Staff Committee is to be established consisting of the chiefs of staff of the permanent members of the Security Council or their representatives, who shall advise and assist the Council in all questions relating to the Council's military requirements, with a view to the maintenance of international peace and security, the employment and command of forces placed at its disposal, and the regulation of armaments and possible disarmament. This committee then is not appointed by the Council but has its own basis of authority and can therefore be termed an *independent subsidiary organ*. Such organs are also styled *special bodies*.

---

25) The use of these terms is arbitrary and so cannot express any fundamental difference.

26) Article 29 and R. of Pr. 28.

27) *Yearbook* 1946—47, 410, 454.

Chapter 5

THE ECONOMIC AND SOCIAL COUNCIL

The main line followed in the functional distribution of competences between the special bodies within the United Nations is that political matters fall to the Security Council, legal matters to the International Court of Justice, and economic and social matters to the Council of that name or, where the administration of trust territories is concerned, to the Trusteeship Council.

The Economic and Social Council, however, occupies a position quite different from that of the Security Council. It is not, like the latter, a primary organ but performs its functions under the authority of the General Assembly (Article 60). Besides acting on its own initiative, it also functions as an executive organ for carrying out, within its competence, the resolutions of the General Assembly, (Article 66 (1)).

On the other hand, the comparatively small Council, comprising 18 states with one representative each, is by no means meant to carry out the enormous, multifarious economic and social work. The specialized tasks are to a great extent distributed among a series of *subsidiary organs (called commissions)*, set up by the Council and controlled by it, in which other states too are represented. Further, the fact is taken into account that there exist a great number of independent international organizations within the UN, each of them charged with certain tasks which by their nature fall within the competence of the Council. In order to avoid duplication of work, the Council's mission is only to bring these organizations, which are then called *specialized agencies,* into relation with the UN. The specialized agencies — apart from the fact that they are not controlled by the Council — function roughly as a group of special bodies for the UN. The Council's own task — beyond its supervising and co-ordinating functions — is then primarily concerned with such matters as are not attended to by the commissions and the specialized agencies.

Composition.

According to Article 61, the Economic and Social Council consists of 18 members of the United Nations elected by the General Assembly (by a two-thirds majority, Article 18) for a period of three years. Each member has one representative who may be joined by deputies and technical advisers if so desired. The Charter does not (in contrast with Article 23) contain any criterion for election, but the natural implication must have been that the industrially important states should be represented on this Council. This means that re-election can take place, which will make it possible for certain important states to become quasi-permanent members.

Scope and Nature of Powers.

The work of the Council is the international economic and social co-operation defined in Article 55 as co-operation for the promotion of

(a) higher standards of living, full employment, and conditions of economic and social progress and development;

(b) solutions of international economic, social, health, and related problems; and international cultural and educational co-operation; and

(c) universal respect for, and observance of, human rights and fundamental freedoms for all without distinction as to race, sex, language, or religion.

In organizational matters it comes within the competence of the Council to set up the necessary subsidiary organs (commissions), to enter into agreements concerning co-operation with governmental organizations and co-ordinate their activities, and to make arrangements for consultation with non-governmental organizations.[1])

The competence of the Council is always merely "advisory". It can never command, at most recommend, cf. Article 62.

As in the case of the General Assembly (cf. above p. 61), three phases may be distinguished within this competence, namely (1) investigation, (2) discussion and criticism, and (3) recommendation. It is expressly stated that the recommending function of the Council may assume the form of drafting conventions (treaties) for submission to the General Assembly, and calling international conferences, Article 62 (3 and 4).

In Article 56 it is said that the members pledge themselves to take joint and separate action in co-operation with the organization for the achievement of the purposes set forth in Article 55 (mentioned above). This of course does not imply that the recommendations of the Economic and Social Council are not in fact recommendations but legally binding; it is merely an extremely vague pledge to assume a "favourable attitude". The members are not even obliged to report on the steps taken to ensure the carrying out of the recommendations of the Council (or of proposals made by the General Assembly concerning matters coming under the competence of the Council), but the Council may make arrangements with the members to obtain such reports, Article 64.

---

1) Articles 68, 63, and 71.

Voting.

Under Article 67 each member has one vote, and resolutions are passed by a majority of the members present and voting. In this quite unpolitical field the great powers have neither voting nor membership privileges (as they have in the Security Council) and no qualified majority is required (as in the Security Council and in important questions in the General Assembly).

Rules of Procedure.

The Council has at least two regular annual sessions but is also to meet at the request by a majority of its members, by the General Assembly or by the Security Council, acting in pursuance of Article 41.

It can invite a member of the UN to participate without vote in the meetings on matters of special interest to that member. It may also make arrangements for representatives of the specialized agencies to take part without vote in the deliberations of the Council as well as of its commissions, Articles 69, 70.

Organization.

In the Economic and Social Council, the work carried out by committees composed of members of the Council is not of the same importance as in the General Assembly.

The rules of procedure contain no indication of *ordinary working committees,* but the Council has set up four such committees:

(1) Committee on negotiations with intergovernmental agencies (the president and eleven members).

(2) Committee on arrangements for consultation with non-governmental organizations (the president and five members).

(3) Agenda committee (the president, the two vice-presidents, and two members).

(4) Interim committee on programme of meetings (the president and five members).

Further, the Council has established various *ad hoc* committees.

Of far greater importance is the right, under Article 68, to establish *subsidiary organs* which are not limited to the circle of the members,[2]) and which in this case are termed *commissions.* Fairly independently, yet under the instruction and supervision of the Council, these commissions attend to various specialized tasks. At present there are nine functional and three regional commissions with a total of 191 members. This affords a possibility of including in the work a large number of states besides those represented in the Economic and Social Council itself, all according to their special interests and qualifications.

These commissions are:

A. Functional commissions:

1. *Economic and employment* (15 members elected in three groups for two, three, and four years respectively). Its function is to study economic problems for the raising of the standard of living. It is especially to deal with questions of economic crises, full employment, reconstruction of devastated areas, the economic development of backward areas.
2. *Transport and communications* (15 members elected in three groups for two, three, and four years respectively).
3. *Statistical* (12 members elected in three groups for two, three, and four years respectively). It is to deal with questions concerning the improvement of the national statistical systems and their correlation, the collection and dissemination of statistical information, and the improvement of statistical methods in general.
4. *Human rights* (18 members elected in three groups for two, three, and four years respectively). It deals with an international declaration of the human rights (not binding) and a regular convention of civil freedoms, freedom of information and the like; further with questions of the protection of minorities and the prevention of discrimination with regard to race, sex, language and religion.
5. *Social* (18 members elected in three groups for two, three, and four years). It deals with social questions in general, particularly such as are not covered by any special agency.

---

2) In the Economic Commission for Asia and the Far East, there are even states which are not members of the UN.

6. *Status of women* (15 members elected in three groups for two, three, and four years respectively). Its subject is the rights of women in a political, economic, and educational respect.
7. *Narcotic drugs* (15 members elected for three years).
8. *Fiscal* (15 members elected in three groups for two, three, and four years respectively). This commission deals with all international financial problems, particularly with their legal, administrative, and technical aspect.
9. *Population* (12 members elected in three groups for two, three, and four years respectively). Its function is to study fluctuations in the populations and their connection with economic and social conditions, as well as questions concerning migrations of populations.

B. Regional commissions.

1. Economic commission for *Europe* (18 members), ECE.
2. Economic commissions for *Asia and the Far East* (13 members).
3. Economic commission for *Latin America* (25 members).

The function of each of these commissions is to deal with the economic problems especially belonging to the regions in question. They are provisional, and the Council for 1951 is to decide whether or not they are to continue.

Connected with the Council are various *independent subsidiary organs (special bodies),* i. e. whose existence is not due to the unilateral resolution of the Council under Article 68, but which have a special legal foundation, giving the Council a certain influence. These are:

1. *The Permanent Central Opium Board* composed of eight persons appointed for five years by the Economic and Social Council in accordance with the provisions of the 1925 convention as amended by the Protocol of December 11, 1946. Its task is the general international supervision of the trade in narcotic drugs.

2. *The Supervisory Body,* which in accordance with the above-mentioned convention is composed of four experts, one appointed by the Commission on Narcotic Drugs, one by the Permanent Central Opium Board, and two by the World Health Organization. Its task is to study the estimates of the requirement of narcotics for medical and scientific purposes of the various countries.

3. *The International Children's Emergency Fund,* ICEF, — established by the General Assembly but reporting to the Economic and Social Council – and the United Nations Appeal for Children, (UNAC).

Above at p. 53—56 we mentioned the number of *specialized agencies* which, by agreement, have been brought into relation with the UN.

Finally the Economic and Social Council is also connected with a large number of *non-governmental international organizations,* e. g. the International Chamber of Commerce, the Inter-Parliamentary Union, the International Law Association, international peace associations, labour organizations, and many others, at present 73 in all.

Chapter 6

THE TRUSTEESHIP COUNCIL

The field of activity of the Economic and Social Council as defined in Article 55[1]) is so extensive that it could seemingly include all economic and social problems, in the widest sense, affecting the government of colonies and former mandated territories established under the Covenant of the League of Nations. These problems are, however, in many respects of a special kind, partly because they are coloured by special ethnographical and cultural conditions, partly because the general question as to the progressive development of the colonial populations towards self-government or complete independence is in a separate class. It has therefore been found desirable to set these problems aside for special treatment and for that purpose a trusteeship system has been established which, however, does not automatically include every colonial territory but only such as have been brought under the system by agreement. Its fundamental idea is that under the agreement the administering authority undertakes the administration, not as a right in its own interest, but as a task for the promotion of the welfare of the local population — in the same way as a guardian acts on behalf of and in the interest of his ward.

But just as there is in the civic community a "public trustee office" or other authorities which keep an eye on guardians to see that they do not abuse their trust for their own

---

1) See above p. 89.

benefit and at the expense of their wards, thus also in international relations — and perhaps even to a greater extent — it is necessary to control the administering authority which has undertaken to act as trustee for another nation.

It is this power of control which the Charter has given to the Trusteeship Council. The latter, however, is only a secondary organ which normally is subject to the authority of the General Assembly,[2] and in special cases to that of the Security Council.[3]

Composition.

Under Article 86 the Trusteeship Council consists of the following members of the UN:

(a) The members which administer trust territories;

(b) such of the permanent members of the Security Council as are not administering trust territories; and

(c) as many other members elected for three-year terms by the General Assembly as are necessary to ensure that the total number of members of the Trusteeship Council is equally divided between those members of the UN which administer trust territories and those which do not.

It may also be expressed as follows. Both as a trustee and as a great power a state is an ex officio member of the council and in addition so many members are elected as will bring about the required balance.

At present six states have entered trusteeship agreements. Consequently the Council has 12 members. Two of the great powers (China and the U.S.S.R.) are not trustees. Hence the number of elected members is four.

Each member of the Council appoints a specially qualified person to represent it in the Council.

---

2) Articles 85 and 87.

3) Namely as far as "strategic areas" are concerned, cf. Articles 82 and 83.

Scope and Nature of Powers.

It is not among the functions of the Trusteeship Council to administer the territories brought under the system. The administration is left to the authority designated by the agreement. Nor is the Council to be a Court of Appeal which can try or alter the administrative authority's decisions. Under Article 76 its sole function is to exercise supervision of the administration of the trust territory. In this supervision the Council is guided by the objectives which according to Article 76 underlie the Trusteeship System, as these may be detailed in the agreement.

Among these aims are mentioned that of "furthering international peace and security". This does not mean that it is the duty of the Council to exercise political functions for the maintenance of peace in accordance with Chapters VI and VII. The task of the Council can never go beyond supervision of the administration, and the only claim made in the passage in question is that this supervision may also aim at such organization of the administration as will promote international peace and security.

As it is, these aims accord well with the general purposes of the UN in the economic and social field, with additions following from the nature of the circumstances, especially the regard for the progressive development of the people in question towards (limited) self-government or (full) independence.

Implicit in the right of "supervision" must be the right of (1) investigation, (2) discussion and criticism, and (3) recommendation, whereas there is no foundation for the Council being able to make binding decisions in any case.

Article 87 specifies that in the exercise of its supervisory function the Council can

a. consider reports submitted by the administering authority;

b. accept petitions and examine them in consultation with the administering authority;
c. provide for periodic visits to the respective trust territories at times agreed upon with the administering authority; and
d. take these and other actions in conformity with the terms of the trusteeship agreements.

Voting.

Each member of the Trusteeship Council has one vote, and decisions are made by a majority of the members present and voting. While the great powers have thus (as in the Security Council) a special privilege of membership, they have no special privilege in voting. Nor is a qualified majority required (as in the Security Council and, in important questions, in the General Assembly).

Rules of Procedure.

The Council meets in two regular sessions each year, convened respectively in January and in June. Special sessions are held by decision of the Council or at the request of various organs or members.[4])

Organization.

The Council may set up such committees as it deems necessary.[5]) The rules of procedure do not prescribe any *ordinary* committees, nor has the Council so far set up any such. On the other hand, it has occasionally appointed *ad hoc* committees, e. g. to make periodic visits to trust territories.

The Council has no right to establish subsidiary organs, i. e. working organs not confined to the circle of members.

4) Rules of Procedure 1 and 2.
5) R. of Pr. 66.

Chapter 7

THE INTERNATIONAL COURT OF JUSTICE

According to Article 92 the International Court of Justice is the principal judicial organ of the United Nations. It is to function in accordance with the annexed Statute which forms an integral part of the Charter.

We cannot here give an account of the provisions of the statute governing the composition and function of the Court. On this point the reader is referred to the exposition in my Textbook of International Law. Here we shall merely offer a few remarks on the position of the Court under the provisions of Chapter XIV of the Charter.

The Dumbarton Oaks proposals expressed no opinion on the position of the Court, but referred the question to a committee of jurists which met at Washington in April, 1945. There was here a difference of opinion on the fundamental question whether the Permanent Court of International Justice, established in 1920 and still existing, should be reorganized, or a formally quite new institution should be created. The latter alternative was chosen by the San Francisco Conference, especially on account of the rules governing the election of the judges and of membership, the name being at the same time changed to the International Court of Justice. The Statute of the new Court is, however, in the main identical with that of the old one.

While the earlier Court's relation to the League of Nations had not been quite clear, it was now established that the Court is an organ of the United Nations and the Statute an integral part of the Charter.

It follows that, as expressly stated in Article 93, each member of the UN is *ipso facto* a party to the Statute of the Court. This does not mean, however, that each member is thus automatically subject to the jurisdiction of the Court. Now as before this requires a special jurisdictional agreement, which, however, can be entered into by a declaration in accordance with Article 36 of the Statute. To facilitate the transition it was also decided, by an addition to Article 36 of the Statute, that declarations made under the old Statute's Article 36 and still in force should be deemed as between the parties to the present Statute to be acceptances of the compulsory jurisdiction of the International Court of Justice for the period which they still had to run and in accordance with their terms.

That each member of the United Nations is ipso facto a party to the Statute therefore only means that, being a member of the United Nations, it is a party to the establishment of the Court and that it has the right to avail itself of the services of the Court, and the duty established by the Statute[1]) to contribute financially towards its expenses.

The Court is not intended to monopolize the members' litigation nor are the members meant to have a monopoly of access to the Court. In the former respect Article 95 states that nothing in the Charter shall prevent members from entrusting the solution of their differences to other courts by virtue of agreements already in existence or to be concluded in the future. In the latter respect Article 93 (2) lays down that a state which is not a member of the UN may become a party to the Statute of the International Court of Justice on conditions to be determined in each case by the General Assembly upon the recommendation of the Security Council. By virtue of this decision Switzerland has become a party to the statute. The conditions required were (1) acceptance of the provisions of the Statute of the Court; (2) acceptance

1) Under Article 33 the expenses of the Court are to be borne by the UN in the manner decided by the General Assembly.

of all the obligations of a member of the United Nations under Article 94 of the Charter (i. e. especially to comply with the decision of the Court in any case to which Switzerland is a party)[2]; (3) an undertaking to contribute to the expenses of the Court.[3]) But the International Court of Justice is even open to states which are not parties to the statute, on conditions determined by the Security Council. The latter has laid down the following conditions: The state in question shall previously have deposited with the registrar of the Court a declaration by which it undertakes, either in reference to a particular dispute or disputes or generally, to accept the same obligations as those above for Switzerland, points 1 and 2. The Court then fixes the contribution to the expenses to be paid by the state concerned in each particular case.[4])

From the fact that the Statute of the Court is an integral part of the Charter it also follows that it can only be amended by the same procedure as is provided in Articles 108 and 109 for the Charter. This is expressly stated in Article 69 of the statute. In Article 70 it is added that the Court shall have power to propose amendments to the Statute through written communications to the Secretary-General. The proposal does not involve any obligation to put it to a vote.

Article 94 offers possibilities of *coercive measures* to give effect to the judgments of the Court. First the self-evident rule is stated that each member is bound to comply with the decision of the Court in any case to which it is a party (as a consequence of having submitted to the jurisdiction of the Court). But further it is laid down that if any state fails to do so the opposite party can submit the case to the

2) The reference is to "all" obligations under Article 94, but it is, I suppose, doubtful whether the latter establishes other obligations than the one pointed out. If the Council makes a decision according to Article 94, it seems to me most correct to say that the obligation to accept and carry it out is established by Article 25. At any rate, Switzerland by accepting all the obligations under Article 94 cannot be deemed to have accepted any obligations to carry out measures against any other state decided by the Security Council.

3) *Yearbook* 1946—47, 595.

4) *Yearbook* 1946—47, 411 and Statute, Article 35.

Security Council which may, if it deems necessary, make recommendations or decide upon measures to be taken to give effect to the judgment. It should be noted that the Council is quite free to decide whether or not it will do anything in the matter. As the decision is made under Article 27 (3), no enforcement of a judgment in the case of a great power will ever come into question.

This provision gives rise to no little doubt.

(1) Has the winning party, if the judgment is not complied with, only recourse to the Security Council, or has it the right to resort to war for the enforcement of its right? The corresponding provision in the Covenant of the League of Nations, Article 13 (4), was interpreted in the latter way. It must probably also be assumed, according to the Charter of the United Nations, that sanctions are excluded against a state whose material right has been established by judgment. In that case — as also when the Council or the General Assembly in a recommendation of peaceful settlement has approved the conduct of a state, cf. below p. 117 — it would seem that the formal judgment as to who is the aggressor must give way to a material evaluation of who is in the right.[5])

(2) Under Article 94 only "the opposite party" has recourse to the Security Council, not the party refusing to comply with the decision of the Court. Even if it is not very likely in the case of a court such as the International Court of Justice, such refusal may be based on the objection that the Court has acted *ultra vires.* If now the winning party appeals to the Security Council and the losing party enters its protest against this, can the Council decide this legal question?

(3) Of more importance is the question as to whether the power of the Council to make "decisions" — which in contrast with "recommendations" must refer to coercive measures according to Chapter VII — goes beyond its powers under Chapter VII or is subject to the conditions laid down in that chapter. The question may also be formulated thus. Does Article 94 give the Council independent powers to order coercive measures so as to give effect to a judgment, or can this only take place as a political measure in so far as non-compliance will give rise to a situation which is a threat to the peace? The preparatory

---

5) Cf. *Constantin Vulcan,* L'exécution des décisions de la Court Internationale de Justice, RGDIP (1947) 187 f.

documents give no conclusive answer to this question. Since Article 94 (2) would have been superfluous according to the latter interpretation, it seems to me most correct to assume, on a formal interpretation, that there is an independent competence. This result is indeed most consistent with the actual facts to be considered (the interest of the small states) and the claims of justice.[6].

Under Article 96 the Court can give an *advisory opinion* on any legal question at the request either of the General Assembly, the Security Council, or of other organs and specialized agencies of the UN authorized by the General Assembly, as far as legal questions arising within their scope are concerned. Such authority has now been given to the Economic and Social Council, the Trusteeship Council, and all the fully established specialized agencies.

---

6) Concurring *F. Blaine Sloan,* Enforcement of Arbitral Awards in International Agencies, 3 Arbitration Journal (1948) 145. *Constantin Vulcan,* l. c., is of the opposite opinion.

Chapter 8

THE SECRETARIAT

At first sight it may seem strange that in Article 7 the Charter refers to the Secretariat as one of the principal organs of the United Nations on a level with the others mentioned in the preceding part.

The characterization would indeed be unwarranted if the Secretariat were merely to be regarded as a clerical departement with no initiative of its own, whose sole function was to report on meetings, make records, dispatch the correspondence of the organization and carry out other similar office work.

This, however, is far from being the case. Article 99, which provides that the *Secretary-General* can bring to the notice of the Security Council any matter which in his opinion may threaten the maintenance of international peace and security, shows quite clearly that the Secretary-General is something more than a mere clerk. He is to have initiative of his own in political questions, really an organic function, which makes him a kind of exalted international inspector. His initiative can be of importance in cases where, for political reasons, the parties implicated in a dispute or situation and outside states hesitate to act as "informers" (Article 35).

Hence it is of importance that the Secretary-General should be not only an able administrative officer but also a prominent personage, able to maintain his position with authority and tact. For this reason the General Assembly resolved prior to the appointment of the Secretary-General that the terms of the appointment should be such as to allow a man of eminence and high attainment to accept the office.[1] Further, the appointment was to be for five years, being open at the end of that period for a further five-year term. And finally the General Assembly, in view of the fact that the Secretary-General was to be a confidant of many governments, thought it desirable that no member should offer him, immediately upon his retirement, any governmental position, and that he for his part should refrain from accepting any such position.[2]

But even apart from Article 99 it has been made possible for the Secretary-General to take initiative. In the rules of procedure for the General Assembly, the Security Council, the Economic and Social Council and the Trusteeship Council[3] the Secretary-General (or his deputies) have been given the right to report orally or in writing upon any subject under discussion. This has given the Secretary-General and his staff an opportunity to exercise considerable influence on the work of the United Nations. That the opportunity only seems to have been used to a slight degree to date is perhaps due to the fact that the attempt of the Secretary-General to intervene in the Iranian affair was a failure, since he then found himself opposed by the majority of the Council.[4] This episode may be supposed to have weakened his inclination to take initiative in the work of the organization; this can only be regretted, for experience would

---

1) The Secretary-General receives an annual salary of $ 20,000, with a further $ 20,000 for representation expenses.

2) *Yearbook* 1946—47, 613—14.

3) Rules 49, 22, 28, and 26 respectively.

4) See also *Yearbook* 1946—47, 332 f. *Clyde Eagleton,* The Jurisdiction of the Security Council over Disputes, Am. J. 40 (1946) 530—31, contends that the Memorandum of the Secretary-General expressed the juridically correct view, and that the rejection of it by the Security Council was due to political considerations.

seem to show the need of a central, impartial inspiration and guidance, not least in the negotiations of the General Assembly. It must be kept in mind, however, that it takes some time to build up the standing and authority he needs if his attempts in this direction are to be successful.

On the other hand, we should be going too far if we regarded the relation between the rest of the organs and the Secretariat as analogous to the relation between a parliament and the executive departments. The Secretariat does not, like the latter, possess any independent executive power. Apart from specific authorization its function is restricted to the influence it may exercise on the resolutions before they are passed, through information and advice.

Nor is any independent specialized competence assigned to the Secretariat on any point — apart from Article 99 — beyond or equal to the competence assigned to the other organs.

It is a matter of course that it is the task of the Secretariat to carry out all the technical office work in connection with the meetings and business of the organization. Examples are: receiving, printing, translating, and distributing documents, reports, and resolutions; translating speeches; writing, translating, and distributing the minutes of the meetings; keeping the documents of the organization; publishing the yearly report; setting up and administering an archive; sending out communications to the members etc. etc.

Considering all these things, it will be most suitable to characterize the Secretariat as an *advisory, subsidiary organ* (established by the Charter itself, and hence *independent*) to serve all the other primary organs except the International Court of Justice (Article 98).

According to the decision of the General Assembly, the Secretariat is organized so as to comprise eight departments, namely:

(1) Department of Security Council Affairs
(2) Department of Economic Affairs

(3) Department of Social Affairs
(4) Department of Trusteeship and Information from non-selfgoverning Territories
(5) Department of Public Information
(6) Legal Department
(7) Conference and General Services
(8) Administrative and Financial Services.

For the special service of the Secretary-General and the co-ordination of the work of the Departments an executive office for the Secretary-General has also been established.

Each of the eight departments are supervised by Assistant Secretaries General, one of whom has the character of a deputy to the Secretary-General.

The Secretary-General is appointed by the General Assembly on the recommendation of the Security Council, Article 97.

The staff is appointed by the Secretary-General under regulations established by the General Assembly, Article 101 (1).

In the performance of their duties the Secretary-General and the staff may not seek or receive instructions from any government or from any other authority outside the organization. They must refrain from any action which might reflect on their position as international officials solely responsible to the organization.

Each member of UN undertakes to respect the exclusively international character of the responsibilities of the Secretary-General and the staff and not to seek to influence them in the discharge of their responsibilities, Article 100.

These provisions do not cancel the nationality of the members of the Secretariat and their subjection to the jurisdiction of their own country. In that sense the Secretariat is not super-national. But the states have undertaken to respect the exclusively international character of the function. This may become important, for instance, if a member of the Secretariat during the performance of his duties as such carries out actions which under the laws of his own country are punishable as treason — e. g. if he takes part in the preparation of plans for military action against his country under Chapter VII. In such a case the obligation under Article 100 (2) will mean that his own country has undertaken not to hold him responsible on that account.

Part III

THE FUNCTIONS OF THE UNITED NATIONS

Chapter 1

ENDS, FUNCTIONS, AND PRINCIPLES

The "Purposes" of the United Nations.

In its first article the Charter of the United Nations contains a statement of the purposes of the organization.

Before proceeding to record the contents of this Article, however, it may be in place to consider the actual aim in indicating the "purposes" of an organization.

It would perhaps be nearest at hand to define the purpose as the ultimate result, the final object, which is desired from the activity of the organization. I will call this the *end* aimed at by the organization, in the same way as it may be said, for instance, that a volunteer fire brigade has been established for the end of fighting fire hazards in a particular district.

In stating the purposes of an organization, however, more than this is usually meant. The statement may also include, in broad outline, the kind of activity, the measures taken by the organization to realize this end, which may perhaps be promoted in many different ways. Fire hazards in a district may be fought not only by providing effective means of extinguishing fires but also by introducing appropriate building practices, by disseminating information about precautionary measures, by penal rules and other arrangements to eliminate the causes of fires. If the article concerning the purposes of the organization is to provide a general framework for and a guide to the activities of the organization, it must not only state the end aimed at but also the ways and means by which it is to be reached. I will call this part of the statement of purposes the *functions* of the organization.

But even though a particular measure is in principle recognized as a means to the end aimed at, this does not mean that it can be carried out under all circumstances and at all costs. For it may well be conceived that, besides promoting the purpose it serves, it may also have other, undesired, effects. When the purpose to be promoted is not regarded as the only value in the world, there will always be the question of weighing it against other values, and of the price that will have to be paid for it. An effective way of fighting fire hazards would no doubt be to prohibit entirely the building of wooden houses, but it is quite possible that this interference with building will be found too high a price to pay. A comprehensive statement of purposes, therefore, should also include an account of the other values to be considered which will restrict freedom of action in the exercise of the organizational functions. I will call this latter part of the statement of purposes the *restrictive principles* of the organization.

The complete scheme indicating the "purposes" of an organization will then be as follows:

The purposes of an organization are
— to the end E
— to perform the functions F_1, F_2 . . . .
— while applying the principles P_1, P_2 . . . .[1])

Even though the provisions concerning the purposes of the Charter have not been drawn up in formal accordance

1) The formula will be complicated if the organization aims at several ends, each with its function. In the same way a particular set of principles may be associated with each function. Examples of the latter case will appear from what follows.

with this scheme, it is not difficult to discover its separate components in Articles 1 and 2.

Ends aimed at by the United Nations.

Under Article 1 (1) these are "*to maintain international peace and security*". That, then, is the ultimate purpose towards which all the activities of the organization are to be directed.[2]) The legal importance of this statement resides in the fact that it is a guide to the interpretation of the succeeding list of functions and to the performance of the functions in practice. It must, then, always be kept in mind that all powers conferred on the different organs have been given for the exclusive purpose of maintaining international peace and security.

The reference in this formulation to "*security*" as an adjunct to "peace" indicates that the object must be not merely the maintainance of peace, so to speak from one day to another, but also to develop the conditions of international intercourse in a way that will afford the greatest assurance that the peace will not be broken, or at least that any breach of the peace will be nipped in the bud and prevented from growing into large proportions. Only then will that "freedom from fear" be realized which was proclaimed as one of the aims of mankind in the Atlantic Charter.

A limitation of the purpose is implied in the fact that only "*international*" peace and security are mentioned. Thus it falls outside the scope of the ultimate aim of the UN to

---

[2]) Formally, it is true, that purpose is only indicated in Article 1 as the aim of the functions mentioned in paragraph 1. It is, however, a justifiable assumption that the functions mentioned in paragraphs 2—4 have been established for the same purpose and not as ends in themselves, cf. Article 55, in which the purpose of the international economic and social co-operation is said to be "the creation of conditions of stability and well-being which are necessary for peaceful and friendly relations among nations."

maintain peace and security within the individual states, cf. the reservation made in Article 2 (7) for "matters essentially within the domestic jurisdiction" of the individual states. This does not warrant the conclusion, however, that every civil war or revolution is extraneous to the organization. That will not be the case if the domestic dissensions in their further consequences involve a danger to the international peace. And this will often be so. Thus the civil war in Spain 1936—39 could not be regarded as merely an internal Spanish affair. But even so it is doubtful whether the conflict can continue to be looked upon as an internal affair if the rebels are able to consolidate themselves as a so-called local insurgent party, establishing itself within a certain region as an organized power under a local *de facto* government. For such a local insurgent party is a subject of international law, though with a limited status. Thus the conflict would seem to have acquired international character. In accordance with these views the Council has laid down that the insurrection in Indonesia cannot be considered merely a domestic Dutch matter.

Functions of the United Nations.

Just as the most obvious task of a fire brigade is to take steps to deal with real or threatened fires, the primary function of the United Nations as a guardian of the peace must be to take steps to combat any real or threatened breaches of the peace. I will call this its *police function.*

In Article 1 (1) this is expressed to the effect that it shall be the purpose of the United Nations (to the end of maintaining international peace and security) *to take effective collective measures for the prevention and removal of threats to the peace and for the suppression of acts of aggression or other breaches of the peace.*

This police function is of a repressive nature, i. e. it turns against the accomplished or threatened breach of the peace and consists in preventing it or removing it by effective means, i. e. coercive measures.

We must not be misled by the fact that "prevention" is also mentioned. The "prevention" here dealt with is essentially different from that which aims at fighting the deep-seated causes that may lead to a breach of the peace. It refers to a situation which has in it the direct germ of a breach of the peace, and it consists of precautions of the same kind as those employed in the event of an actual breach of the peace, i. e. coercive measures. It is the same sort of thing that happens as when the police not only arrest the thief caught in the act, but also the person who is preparing to commit a burglary.

Essentially different, on the other hand, are the actual preventive measures. These are directed against conditions which, according to general experience, may be feared sooner or later to cause a breach of the peace, and they do not in any case consist of coercive measures, but in judicial and social regulations. Here two stages may be distinguished: first that connected with the external and immediate causes of war; secondly that connected with the more deepseated and intangible factors which may lead to a breach of the peace.

The immediate cause of a war will normally be a dispute between the parties, and the first and most "superficial" of the preventive measures must consist in arrangements for settling disputes between states *(the settling function).* It is expressed in Article 1 in the passage *"by peaceful means to bring about .... adjustment or settlement of international disputes or situations which might lead to a breach of the peace"*. (By situations we must understand conflicts between states in which the opposed interests have not yet been expressed in such precisely formulated demands and claims that it can be described as a "dispute". "The situation", if it is not adjusted, will normally pass into a "dispute" and thus lies at a deeper level in the causal connection than a "dispute").

When finally we come to the deep-seated causes of strife and war, that is, to the conditions that give rise to conflicts (situations and disputes) between states, opinions as to these are so divided that the most diverse measures for the prevention of war can be based on these different views. There are, for instance, those who think that the capitalist system of production will necessarily lead to war, and that the object therefore must be to try to abolish this and replace it by a socialistic economic system. Others think that only a change of heart in harmony with the ideals of the Christian faith can bring about peace in the world. Others again contend that the deepest cause is in the political structure of the world with its multiplicity of fully sovereign states, and think that the way to peace must be by the establishment of a world state. Various other theories have been advanced according to which the root of the evil is to be found in deep-seated irrational factors of a psychological, biological (particularly sexual), economic, political or social nature.

The Charter of the United Nations, in its measures for the prevention of war, has not based its provisions on any of these problematical theories which chiefly indicate irrational factors as the causes of war. Without committing itself to a definite theory the Charter in the main keeps to the obvious fact that distress, misery and social insecurity are conditions favoring unrest and war. You may then interpret this fact in terms of rational motives, saying that men wage war from dire necessity, i.e. because of the insufficient satisfaction of various (not merely economic) needs, and in the hope of being able to secure advantages to themselves at the expense of others by the use of force. Or you may prefer with the social psychologists to assume that frustation of needs leads to aggressiveness, the target of the aggression often being unrelated to the source of frustation. "People who are thwarted in their everyday needs for subsistence, economic security, personal status, self-expression, etc., may become aggressive, and this aggression may frequently be directed at accessible and socially approved targets, such as 'foreigners' or 'enemy countries'."[2a]) In either case it is true that the distress could be fought down more effectively if the states, instead of working each in its own interest, united in co-operation for the promotion of common interests; and that at the same time one of the causes leading to war would be abolished.

It is, then, the sustaining idea in the United Nations' programme for the prevention of war that the most important object (besides the settlement of disputes) is to promote as much international co-operation as possible for the promotion of the common interest in all areas of social life. If it is possible in this way to bring about freedom from distress, one of the chief causes of war will have been removed from the world.

In Article 1 (3) of the Charter this function — *the function of co-operation* — is thus expressed: "*to achieve international co-operation in solving international problems of an economic, social, cultural, or humanitarian character*", cf. Article 55 (a and b), where the same aim is described in more detail.

It may be doubtful whether the questions whose solution is here under discussion can appropriately be characterized as "international". It may easily suggest a conflict in interests. Such questions as improvement of the standards of living, full employment, and conditions of economic and social progress and development (Article 55 (a)) are not primarily international but national questions. At best they become international when they are dealt with through international co-operation.

The basic view here outlined has been taken over from the League of Nations. On one point only has the Charter gone beyond it and taken into consideration *an irrational*

[2a]) *David Krech and Richard S. Crutchfield,* Theory and Problems of Social Psychology (1948) 587—88.

cause of war, namely the dissolution of that moral and legal respect for the individual which is expressed more fully in the traditional doctrine of human rights and the fundamental freedoms. It was this distintegration of a Christian-humanistic tradition and the cynical profession of a belief in brute force which set the Fascist states apart. Closely related to this are race myths and race hatred. The Charter of the United Nations is based on the idea that a mentality of this type is a danger to peaceful intercourse between the nations and that it must therefore be one of the tasks of the organization to try to reinstate humanistic ideals in men's minds and to make the legal claims based on them respected in the international Community.

In accordance with these ideals it is stated in Article 1 (3) to be one of the functions of the organization "*to achieve international co-operation . . . in promoting and encouraging respect for human rights and for fundamental freedoms for all without distinction as to race, sex, language, or religion.*"

In this connection we may also cite the preamble to the constitution of UNESCO where the same idea has found a fuller and more forcible expression:

"The Governments of the States parties to this Constitution on behalf of their peoples declare

that since wars begin in the minds of men it is in the minds of men that defences of peace must be constructed,

that the great and terrible war which has now ended was a war made possible by the denial of the democratic principles of the dignity and mutual respect of men and by the propagation, in their place, through ignorance and prejudice, of the doctrine of the inequality of men and races . . . and

that a peace based exclusively upon the political and economic arrangements of governments would not be a peace which could secure the unanimous lasting and sincere support of the peoples of the world, and that the peace must therefore be founded, if it is not to fail, upon the intellectual and moral solidarity of mankind . . . .".

The function here referred to is a ramification of the co-operative function, distinguished by the fact that its aims conform to the psychological prerequisites of the peace.

In addition to the specific functions set forth here, Article 1 (2) contains a vague general clause. It is there laid down as a purpose (function) "to develop friendly relations among nations .... and to take other appropriate measures to strengthen universal peace." Since, however, in the chapters that follow the competence of the various organs has been specifically defined with the sole exception of that of the General Assembly, the general clause only has importance in relation to the latter organ.

Finally it is stated in Article 1 (4) as a "purpose" of the United Nations that it is to be "a center for harmonizing the actions of nations in the attainment of these common ends." This indicates no new function in the above-mentioned sense. This "purpose" is merely a declaration that organized co-operation has been established by the Charter for the performance of the aforementioned functions to the aforementioned end.

The preamble of the Charter contains a statement of the purposes of the United Nations in more ideologically coloured turns of phrase, which in all essentials correspond to the statements in Article 1. Even though the preamble of a treaty must in principle be regarded as a binding part of the treaty,[3] in the present instance there can hardly be any doubt that for purposes of interpretation the more precise provisions in Article 1 and in the subsequent articles establishing the functions of the individual organs are to take precedence over the preamble.

The Restrictive Principles of the United Nations. — 1. Respect for the Principles of Justice and International Law.

"Munich" has become the symbol of a policy which unscrupulously throws a small state to the wolves in the hope of thus buying "peace in our time". Is it permissible for the United Nations to act on that principle or does law and

[3] In a number of decisions the Permanent Court of International Justice has given the preamble of a treaty constitutive significance equal in principle with its articles, see e. g. the *Lotus judgment* (Publ. de la CPI, Series A, No. 10 p. 17); advisory opinion No. 2 concerning *the competence of ILO*, Series B, No. 2/3 p. 25 f.); advisory opinion No. 13 on the same subject (Series B, No. 13, p. 15, 18, 23).

justice set a limit to the price at which peace may be bought? The question was clearly posed at the San Francisco Conference and the result was a divided answer, as indicated in Article 1 (1). In the performance of their function for the settlement of disputes the United Nations are restricted by consideration for the "principles of justice and international law", but they are not so restricted in the performance of their police function, i. e. as far as enforcement action for the maintenance of peace is concerned.

The view dictating this answer to the problem is that maintenance of order and the settlement of the underlying dispute are two different things. Once the peace has been broken it is the first task of the Security Council to separate the quarrelling parties and restore peace, without being hampered by any consideration as to which party is in the right. The task of the Council is here quite the same as that of the police. The police too separate and apprehend the parties to a fight without first investigating which is the culprit. Thus an aggressive state cannot paralyze the Council's activities for the maintenance of peace by asserting that it is in the right. (An exception must no doubt be made in case the material right has been authoritatively recognized either by judgment or by the Council itself (or the General Assembly) in a recommendation for a pacific settlement, cf. p. 102 and p. 142). On the other hand, as we shall presently see[4]) the Council is not bound to direct its coercive measures against the aggressor. These are not — like those of the League of Nations — in principle "sanctions". The Council is only bound by considerations of effectiveness (Article 1 (1)), but on the other hand, within these bounds it is not cut off from considering the legal aspect, i. e. it is free, all things considered, to do what it thinks best to counteract the breach of the peace at hand.

---

4) Below, p. 141.

As to settling the dispute, the reference to "the principles of justice and international law" cannot mean that the settlement is to take place on the same basis as an actual judicial decision. This would lead to absurd results, especially in the case af political disputes. It is merely intended that the general conception of justice should be taken into account on the same lines as what is usually called a decision *ex æquo et bono*.[5])

It should be noted that considerations of justice must also be taken into account in the relations between individual members in pacific settlement of disputes, Article 2 (3).

The Restrictive Principles of the United Nations. — 2. The Principle of Sovereignty.

Under Article 2 (1) the organization is based on the principle of the sovereign equality of all its members. Linguistically the expression "sovereign equality" is not a happy one. It is not "equality" which sustains the character of sovereignty, but the states. "Equality as sovereign states" is obviously what is meant.

This implies in the first place a recognition of the principle of sovereignty as the fundamental principle of the organization, and it is that aspect of the matter which will be treated in the present section.

In addition to this general reference to the principle of sovereignty the Charter contains in Article 2 (7) a provision which is a special application of the principle. Hence we shall discuss that provision first and thereafter revert to the general principle.

Since an interpretation of Article 2 (7) is impossible without considering its prototype in the Covenant of the League of Nations Article 15 (8) and the equivalent provision in the Dumbarton Oaks Proposals, Chapter VIII, Section A 7,

---

5) Cf. *Ross*, International Law, § 59 IV.

these texts, to which we shall frequently refer, will first be quoted.

> *Covenant Article 15, par. 8:* If the dispute between the parties is claimed by one of them, and is found by the Council, to arise out of a matter which by international law is solely within the domestic jurisdiction of that party ("laisse à la compétence exclusive de cette Partie"), the Council shall so report, and shall make no recommendation as to its settlement.
>
> *Dumbarton Oaks Ch. VIII A, 7:* The provisions of paragraphs 1 to 6 of section A should not apply to situations or disputes arising out of matters which by international law are solely within the domestic jurisdiction of the state concerned.
>
> *Charter, Article 2 (7):* Nothing contained in the present Charter shall authorize the United Nations to intervene in matters which are essentially within the domestic jurisdiction of any state or shall require the members to submit such matters to settlement under the present Charter; but this principle shall not prejudice the application of enforcement measures under Chapter VII.

Three questions will now arise:

(a) What are the circumstances justifying the plea of "domestic jurisdiction" or "reserved matters"?

(b) What are the legal effects of this plea, if justified?

(c) Who is to decide whether or not such a plea is justified?

As to (a). As already mentioned, the model for Article 2 (7) is Article 15 (8) of the Covenant. That provision has a history of its own. President Wilson, during a journey to the U.S. after the first draft for the Covenant had observed that American public opinion was strongly opposed to League intervention in matters regarded as purely American. The questions in view were especially tariffs, immigration, citizenship, race discrimination, and the distribution of raw materials. Owing to that opinion President Wilson caused Article 15 (8) to be inserted — even this, however, was not enough to secure the ratification of the Senate.

Now there is this strange thing about Article 15 (8) that though the practical aim of the provision is fairly clear, the text is based on a theory which is quite untenable. Obviously the intention is to safeguard the states against the possibility that the Council, in a matter in which International Law does not impose any restriction on the liberty of the states, recommends a solution (for the settlement of a dispute) which nevertheless — *ex æquo et bono* or from purely political opportunism — restricts liberty of action. The aim of the provision is then to preserve the spheres in which International Law, as it exists today, gives unlimited liberty of action to the states.

Now this aim is supposed to be expressed in paragraph 8 in the statement that the decisive thing is whether the matter comes within the state's own or sole competence (jurisdiction). The idea is that there are certain matters which by their nature are purely national and therefore outside the competence of International Law. The idea of such a division of competences between International Law and Internal Law is of course — as has often been shown — quite illusory. The implication would be a judicial system superior to both, which does not exist. Every "internal" matter, particularly all the examples cited, which can give rise to a conflict of interests between states, may be conceived to be subject to international regulation. Every formation of new customary law, and especially every new treaty in these domains, affords an example that international law is worming its way into a sphere which was previously free.

The mistake then is that Article 15 (8) speaks of "a question that under international law is solely within the domestic jurisdiction of that party", instead of speaking of "*a question in which the party, under international law, has unlimited liberty of action.*"

But something more is involved than a mere problem of formulation. When we understand the matter properly we see two important consequences.

First, the sphere of the so-called "domaine reservé" is not absolute but *in a double sense relative*. It is relative in view of the general progressive development of international law. Thus, for instance, previously but not now, a state's treatment of aliens was one of the matters which were not subject to international regulation. Further, it varies from state to state according as there exist, or do not exist, treaties concerning the matter.

Second, the question as to whether or not a certain matter comes under the reserved domain cannot be settled by simple consideration of "the nature" of that matter. The question is in itself a *legal* question, often very difficult, the reply to which depends on a thorough examination of international rules of customary law as well as treaty law.

The practical interpretation of Article 15 (8) expounded here has been approved by the Permanent Court of International Justice in the case of the nationality decrees in Tunis and Morocco.[6])

On this point, the Dumbarton Oaks Proposals took over the formulation from the Covenant unaltered.

The final formulation of Article 2 (7), on the other hand, contains the change that it is no longer required that the matter be solely within the domestic jurisdiction of a state. It is enough that the matter is *essentially* within this jurisdiction. ("Compétence nationale d'un État" instead of "compétence exclusive de cette partie").

The above must mean that a protest may be entered if the state in the main has liberty of action in the case in question, and regardless whether there are certain non-essential restrictions of its liberty under International Law.

That change, however, is far from being an improvement. On the contrary, it not only introduces great uncertainty in its application but downright absurdities, which can hardly have been realized.

The main point is that while it is reasonable to maintain,

---

6) Permanent Court of International Justice, Series B No. 4, p.p. 22 ff.

with Article 15 (8), that the Council should not intervene in a matter if the party concerned has an internationally approved right to act as it pleases, it is entirely devoid of reason to exclude the competence of the United Nations in a question which is subject to a certain amount of international regulation. It must be irrelevant that in other respects the matter is essentially one in which the state enjoys liberty of action.

With a view to the requirement of essentiality Article 2 (7) may be analyzed as follows. The insertion of this requirement must, unlike the earlier formulation, imply that the matters are not to be judged on the basis of the concrete dispute at hand but as an exemplification of a certain type of case. For in the concrete case the requirement insisted on must either be justified or not justified. The idea must be that the matter at hand which gives rise to the dispute should be regarded as belonging, for instance, to the type "questions of nationality", "questions of immigration", "questions of the formulation of private international law" etc. etc.. The object will then be to decide whether or not the type of matter in question can be said in the main to be subject to international regulation. How this question is answered must again depend partly on the number of demonstrable international norms of various kinds (pertaining to customary law, to treaty law etc.) which apply to the case, partly on the weight of the interference with freedom of action which is here exemplified. We may expect the following consequences.

First, the decision will to a disagreeable extent be arbitrary. How can international norms be counted or weighed? The flood-gates will be opened to capriciousness and controversy, with the added risk that the application of the article will become a question of politics, not of justice. The uncertainty is further increased by the fact that it will often be quite arbitrary under what category a concrete situation will be considered to fall. Is a dispute concerning a person's right to immigrate under a treaty of immigration and settlement to be referred to the category "questions of immigration", "the legal position of aliens" or "interpretation of treaties"? As we know, the concrete can always be classified under the abstract in many ways.

Second, if we are concerned with a type which — as e. g. "questions of nationality" or "questions on conflicts of law" — in the main has not been regulated by international law, but where there is, precisely in the case of this state, a *single treaty* regulating the question at issue, the organization cannot — as it previously could — base its competence on this solitary norm, for the matter is essentially one of those in which the state has liberty of action. But if the quarrel turns upon this very treaty it is quite absurd to declare the organization incompetent. The same is true of course of the individual norm which has another source than a treaty.

The reason stated at the Conference for inserting the word "essentially" instead of "solely" was "that the word 'solely' is inadequate as a test in view of the fact that under modern conditions what one nation does domestically almost always has at least some external repercussions".[7] This remark seems to imply that the interpretation is concerned with the category and not with the concrete case. But that implication is unnecessary. If it is given up there are no grounds for the otherwise highly unreasonable change.

The consequences of the change are so downright absurd that in my opinion it is necessary, in the name of reason, to *disregard* the essentiality requirement and instead of "essentially" read "solely" in Article 2 (7) and then apply the interpretation to the concrete case, not to the category.

Further Article 2 (7) differs both from Article 15 (8) of the Covenant and from Dumbarton Oaks Chapter VIII A, by the fact that *the reference to international law* as a standard for judgment *has been omitted*. In support of this it was stated that the rules of international law are too vague to serve as an acceptable guide.[8] But what then is to be substituted? A political interpretation will be still more uncertain and arbitrary. As it is, the result — presumably contrary to the intention — will be to narrow down rather than to extend the scope of the objections. The result of a political interpretation will easily be that the matter — whether or not there is international liberty of action in respect of it — will not be regarded as coming under the reserved domain, because in view of its political importance there ought to be a limitation on the liberty of action. But it can hardly be conceived to justify the opposite result. The

---

7) *Goodrich and Hambro,* 74.

8) Op. cit., 74.

practice is in accordance with this. The General Assembly as well as the Security Council have repeatedly refused to let the question of competence be decided by the International Court of Justice. This it has done precisely on the view that the question is not only legal but also political, and for fear that a purely legal decision would exclude the competence of the organization. In the Spanish as well as the Indonesian case the organization would seem to have started from the conception that a question — whatever the result of a purely legal judgment — cannot be regarded as a matter of essentially domestic concern, if politically it gives rise to a dispute or a situation the continuance of which is likely to endanger the maintenance of international peace and security.[9])

In deciding whether a certain matter is subject to the national jurisdiction of a state, i. e. is a matter in which the state has unlimited liberty of action, the United Nations' Charter itself must also be taken into consideration. Hence in matters legally regulated by the Charter so as to impose definite obligations on the members (apart from the obligation to seek the settlement of disputes) the reservation can never be pleaded as an excuse for denying the competence of the organization. Such matters are then no longer merely national. But this recourse to the Charter cannot be carried so far as to exclude appeal to Article 2 (7) on the ground that the case in question comes under the competence of the organization according to the other provisions of the Charter. In that way all limits to the competence of the organization in "national questions" would fall away, and Article 2 (7) would be quite devoid of meaning.

As to (b). The effect of a matter coming within the reserved domain is

(1) that the United Nations, i. e. each of its organs, are incompetent to intervene in the matter, apart from the application of enforcement measures under Chapter VII.

---

9) Cf. *Goodrich,* The United Nations and Domestic Jurisdiction, *Intern. Org.* III (1949) 26, cf. 20, 23. *Dons,* Is the Question of Human Rights a Domestic Matter, *Jus Gentium* I (1949) 77.

(2) that the state in question is not bound to submit the matter to settlement under the Charter.

With regard to the first point, it has obviously been *intended* to give the plea of domestic jurisdiction a broader application of more fundamental importance than was the case according to the Covenant and the Dumbarton Oaks Proposals. In these the protest could only be brought before the Council of the League of Nations and the Security Council respectively in reference to their activities for the settlement of disputes. At the San Francisco Conference the provision was moved from the chapter dealing with the pacific settlement of disputes to the introductory articles concerning general principles, so that in principle it can be resorted to against any organ in the performance of any function. The only limitation left then is the positive reservation with respect to coercive measures and the expression "*intervene*". The question then arises as to what is implied in the latter term.

It would be tempting[10]) to believe that the expression refers to the well-known international concept "intervention", by which is usually meant dictatorial interference in the affairs of another state. However, it is quite clear that this cannot be meant here. On the one hand, the intention is beyond all doubt (cf. the historical evolution) that it should be possible to enter a protest against the activities of the organization for the peaceful settlement of disputes. But that activity can never go beyond making recommendations for voluntary acceptance and is not therefore of a dictatorial kind. On the other hand, it must be equally clear that Article 2 (7) is not meant to be used as a protection against an injunction to the members from the Security Council to use enforcement measures owing to a breach of

10) With *H. Lauterpacht*, Report. Intern. Law Ass. Brussels Conference 1948: Human Rights, the Charter of the United Nations, and the Intern. Bill of Rights of Man, p. 18.

the peace. For if so, the whole security system of the Charter would be overthrown. But these injunctions actually do interfere dictatorially in the internal affairs of the members, in their economic and military systems.

There is hardly any reason to attempt a definition in principle of the expression "intervene", since a casuistic analysis of the various possibilities will furnish sufficient clarity.

On the one hand it is obvious that a protest can be entered against the activity of the Security Council or the General Assembly for *the pacific settlement* under Chapter VI. On the other hand, it has been positively established that the measures taken by the Security Council under *Chapter VII* fall outside the range of objections concerning reserved matters. That is to say then, that if the way in which a state organizes its domestic matters involves a threat to the peace, consideration for liberty of action and "sovereignty" must yield to the interests of peace. The Council can then intervene with coercive measures. Finally, as already mentioned, it is obvious that objections cannot be raised to the *Council's* injunction to proceed to such measures under Chapter VII.

As a doubtful area there remains only the *non-political activity* displayed in the social and economic field by the General Assembly, the Economic and Social Council, and the Trusteeship Council.

In favour of the assumption that protests can be entered in these cases is the consideration that has led to the abovementioned shifting of the provision. The purpose was simply to make it a general principle, not limited to the function of adjusting disputes. Further it may be mentioned that at the conference at San Francisco, in connection with the drafting of the rules concerning the activity of the Economic and Social Council, the following statement was inserted in the report by the committee in question (II/3):

> "The members of Committe 3 of Commission II are in full agreement that nothing contained in Chapter IX (Chapters IX and X of the Charter) can be construed as giving authority to the Organization to intervene in the domestic affairs of member states."[11]

Nevertheless this is unacceptable. The matters meant to fall among the economic and social activities of the organization — standard of living, employment, health and cultural conditions etc. — will to a great extent be decidedly "reserved matters". A right — as in the adjustment function — to enter a protest under Article 2 (7), in the case also of mere proposals, would therefore practically render impossible the work in these spheres.

Nor, we may take it, has this been intended. As spokesman for the sponsoring powers John Foster Dulles said at the Conference that the intention in making Article 2 (7) applicable to the economic and social field too, was to require the organization to deal with the governments and not to penetrate directly in the domestic life of the member states.[12] But interpreted in this way the application of Article 2 (7) becomes *superfluous,* because the Charter opens no way at all in these fields for dictatorial intervention but in all cases calls for negotiation and voluntary action.

On the other hand, it also seems difficult to assume that Article 2 (7) should be without any importance whatever in the economic and social domain. The most reasonable assumption is probably that "intervention" is present when *a recommendation is pointedly directed towards a particular country.*[13] The question is not seen to have been definitively settled in practice.[14]

11) *Goodrich and Hambro,* 191.

12) UNCIO, vol. VI, 508.

13) Thus also *Dons,* Is the Question of Human Rights a "Domestic Matter"?, *Jus Gentium* I (1949) 82.

14) In the second part of the third session of the General Assembly the question of the competence of the Assembly as to the *treatment of*

The other effect mentioned in Article 2 (7) expressly refers only to the obligation to submit disputes for settlement. It means that the state in question is released from the obligation under Article 2 (3) and Article 33 (1) to seek a solution by appropriate means in direct relation to the other party, and is also released from the obligation under Article 37 (1), if mutual agreement is not reached, to refer the matter to the Security Council.

The complete exemption from all measures for reconciliation which follows from the rules of paragraphs 1 and 2 does not mean, however, that the state should therefore have the right to assert its views and interests by force. That is categorically excluded by Article 2 (4). Raising the objection only means that the question is kept in abeyance in the usual political game among the states, with the usual pressures which may be brought to bear.

What are the interests behind these reservations for domestic affairs? Why are the states, particularly the great powers, so anxious to safeguard their "sovereignty" on this

---

Indians in South Africa and the *trials of church leaders in Hungary and Bulgaria* was hotly debated. In both cases the defending state denied the competence of the organization, maintaining that any discussion of the matter would be an intervention within the meaning of Article 2 (7). But although resolutions commenting upon the matter were carried in both cases, and although the views of the majority were partly based on the assumption that Article 2 (7) does not forbid a recommendation pointedly directed at a particular country, no definite conclusion may be drawn from those instances. The resolutions in both cases refer also to obligations under special treaties, and the implication may be that for this reason the matters concerned are not questions within the domestic jurisdiction of the states (*Bulletin*, VI (1949) 416 f., 480 f. and 576 f.). The same holds true in the case concerning *Soviet wives of foreign citizens* in which the question was raised again. In this case the position of the majority was partly founded on the assertion that the Soviet Union action involved a violation of traditional practice with regard to diplomatic immunities (l. c., 522).

point, and to preserve their liberty of action? Why do they oppose every obligation to seek or comply with the settlement of disputes in this field?

Since "reserved matters", according to the definition, are such in which international law justifies unlimited liberty of action, their fear cannot be a fear of subjecting the dispute to a purely legal judgment. For in the given circumstances this could only be in favour of the state raising the objection. Hence the only possibility to be feared would be that the settlement *ex æquo et bono* would end in decisions going beyond what current international law now demands. Hence the idea behind Article 2 (7) is an interest in preserving international law at its present stage and opposing a further development of it through the efforts of the United Nations to regulate those things which are now abandoned, in anarchistic fashion, to the struggle for political power.

It is not difficult to determine which group of states is interested in this. The major powers alone can reap benefit from asserting the sovereignty principle and lawlessness at the expense of the competence of the United Nations to adjust disputes and a further development of international law. From a legal point of view, Article 2 (7) is *the quintessence of the tendency of the sovereignty dogma to resist progress.* But by the very act of investing the craving for power with the alluring draperies of this ideology they have succeeded in dazzling the small states — which have a natural desire to be recognized as "sovereign" too — and making them accept a standpoint at variance with their own interests and the claims of law.

Imagine a dispute in which a small state sets up a claim against a great power with respect to one of the "reserved matters" of the latter. The great power is interested in entering a protest under Article 2 (7). That means that all discussion concerning a pacific settlement is cut off and that the question is given over to power politics, which again means that the small state has no chance of being heard.

If, on the contrary, the reverse is the case, it is at any rate doubtful whether it will do the small state any good to plead the reservation of "domestic matters". It will then only be exposed to political pressure. In most cases it will presumably have better chances if it submits the matter to the international organization for settlement.

As to (c). While Article 15 (8) of the Covenant expressly established that the Council was to decide whether the protest was justified, a similar provision has been omitted from the Dumbarton Oaks proposals as well as from Article 2 (7). This circumstance might be taken to indicate that it should be the right of every state definitely to establish what matters were domestic.

Such a solution would, however, be catastrophic. It would mean that the obligation to seek, and submit to, settlement under the Charter of the UN would be just as insubstantial as the obligations under the arbitration treaties of former days with reservations for honour, independence, and vital interests. It would always be possible for a state arbitrarily to elude every obligation.

But the conclusion is unjustified as well. From the history of the origin and evolution of the Charter it appears that no one has thought of it. The omission of an authorization for the powers of the organization is merely due to the fact that the members could not agree as to whether the decision should be in the hands of the organization itself or should lie with the International Court.[15]) Hence the only choice is between these alternatives. In the absence of a positive authorization for the powers of the International Court we must fall back on the generally recognized rule that an organ must itself decide the extent of its competence.

The result will be that if a protest is brought before one of the organs of the UN it must be *the organ itself that*

---

15) See *Kopelmanas*, L'organisation, I, 242.

definitely decides whether or not the protest is justified by the circumstances. This is indeed the practice that has been adopted.

If the protest is brought before the Security Council the *veto rule* will come into operation, since the question can hardly be characterized as procedural. At all events, any of the great powers may compel that result by vetoing the characterization of the question as procedural, cf. the rule in the "Statement", point II.[16])

Through this rule of voting the practical scope of Article 2 (7) is greatly limited, no doubt in an unanticipated way. The opposition of a single great power will render it impossible to put through the protest.[17])

If it is brought before the General Assembly, the Economic and Social Council or the Trusteeship Council the matter is decided by simple majority, cf. Article 18, so here the chance of the protest being heard is considerably greater.

Summing up, it may be said about the reservation in Article 2 (7) of the "domestic jurisdiction" of the states that the provision is extremely vague. Theoretically it rests on the mistaken notion that certain matters are by their nature outside the competence of international law. Practically it expresses an interest, hostile to progress, in preserving political power by retaining the asocial character of international law and the liberty of action it fosters. The introduction of the essentiality qualification, and the omission of a reference to international law as a basis of judgment, tend to replace legal judgment by political judgment. Free play is thereby given to a far-reaching exercise of discretion and to arbitra-

16) See above p. 82.

17) Concording *Kopelmanas,* l. c., 244—45; *Goodrich and Hambro,* 120, contrastingly contend that Article 27 (3) allows a permanent member to prevent action from being taken on the ground that Article 2 (7) would be violated.

riness, at the expense of the interests of justice. The practical scope of the provision is, however, greatly limited by the power of the organization itself to decide whether or not the plea of domestic jurisdiction is justified. In the most important cases when the question arises before the Security Council, the right of veto may be used against acceptance of the plea. This circumstance tends to lend further support to the political character of the judgment. Article 2 (7) on account of its vagueness will often be a well-suited instrument for any party seeking to elude the authority of the organization. It has given and will presumably still give rise to much dissension. As already mentioned, the trend in practice has been to avoid efforts at a legal interpretation of Article 2 (7), and to assert the competence of the organization on a political basis. But it must be noted that in those cases the interests of great powers have not been involved.

Article 2 (7), as previously stated, is a special manifestation of the principle of the "sovereign equality" of the members on which, according to Article 2 (1), the organization is based, and which under Article 78 is also to apply to direct relations between the members. The question will then be what — beyond Article 2 (7) — is implied in this as far as the *principle of sovereignty* is concerned.

The implication is that each member on entering the organization possesses a certain measure of sovereignty (self-government). This follows from the fact that only states can be members, cf. above, p. 43. On that assumption it is established

(1) that the organization is *not* so constituted that it *cancels or limits the sovereignty of the member states,* i. e. that it has not on the model of a federal state established a central authority which independently of the participating states may act as a legislative or other legal body towards the

citizens. The authority of the organization is in all cases of an international character, i. e. it deals directly only with states, the citizens being affected merely after a conversion (perhaps automatic) into national law has taken place. This aspect of the principle is clearly declaratory, i. e. it recognizes the remaining provisions of the Charter which fully bear out the truth of the declaration;

(2) that the member states, unaffected by the Charter, shall continue to enjoy the same *rights* and be subject to the same *obligations* which under common international law apply to "sovereign" states. According to the general theory of sovereignty,[18]) which must be supposed to have animated the authors of the Charter, various "internal and external sovereign rights" accrue from sovereignty, particularly the right freely to determine all "domestic matters" and the claim to respect for the person and territory of the state. For purposes of interpretation it is unnecessary to discuss the fact that it is an illusion to believe that anything at all can be deduced from "sovereignty" as such, and that the actual fact is that the rights (and duties) here in question are simply such as belong to any state under international law without any qualifications beyond its mere existence as a state (its "sovereignty"), also called the fundamental rights and obligations of states. The telling point for interpretation is merely that it is this complex of rights and duties which was meant. This appears from the report of Committee I/1, according to which the following elements are inherent in the sovereignty principle:

> (1) that each state enjoys the right inherent in full sovereignty;
> (2) that the personality of the state is respected as well as its territorial integrity and its political independence; and
> (3) that the state should, under international order, comply faithfully with its international duties and obligations.[19])

---

18) Cf. *Ross,* International Law § 3.
19) *Yearbook* 1946—47, 19.

This corroboration of "sovereign rights" *cannot, however, be taken as a precept* binding for the interpretation of the remaining provisions of the Charter. On several points the Charter establishes far-reaching obligations which are incompatible with that liberty of conduct and independence which in the general view accrue to sovereign states. Not only are the states bound to act upon the commands of the Security Council, even with regard to placing military forces at disposal, but under given circumstances they must also tolerate the application of coercive measures against themselves.

Hence this aspect of the sovereignty principle is also merely declaratory. It is declared that in the main the Charter does not really curtail the current "sovereign rights". Legally Article 2 (1) is without any importance whatever. The purpose of the provision is *political.* Precisely because the Charter on certain points encroaches on what is traditionally associated with the sovereignty ideology the sponsors have felt impelled, as a reassurance, to insert a fundamental (but non-binding) confirmation of the sovereignty principle as one of the first maxims of the Charter.

The Restrictive Principles of the UN. — 3. The Equality Principle.

Special care has been taken to establish the equality principle, i. e. the principle of the equal legal status of the states irrespective of their size, in the Charter (Preamble, Article 1 (2), Article 2 (1), Article 55 (1), Article 78). But the privileges of the major powers — both as to the membership in the Security Council and the Trusteeship Council and as to voting procedure in the Security Council and amendments to the Charter — are palpable and far-reaching violations of the principle. It is obvious that here too we are only concerned with an ideologically motivated declaratory principle in flagrant conflict with the actual facts.

The Restrictive Principles of the UN. — 4. The Self-determination of Peoples.

By Article 1 (2) this principle is established as a guide for the organization and by Article 55 for the relations of members to each other. As generally understood it has several bases.

In a *territorial* respect it means a right for a people or a group (in a sociologico-ethnographical sense) to determine the national dependency of the territory inhabited. On the positive side this would mean a right to claim territorial changes in accordance with the wishes of the population; on the negative side it would mean that no territory could be ceded unless confirmed by a plebiscite.

It is, however, quite impossible to define by any precise or rational criterion the group to which this right should belong. Consistently applied, the principle would demand that the same right should be given to minorities within minorities (e. g. Northern Ireland within Ireland) and so forth, until each house or each farm could decide to what state it would belong. It is obvious that this is nonsense. Legally, therefore, the principle is without substance. At most it may be regarded as a moral and political guide in a negative sense, i. e. it might be required that territorial changes should be confirmed by a plebiscite. This consideration prevented the victors in the First World War from appropriating the German colonies, but induced them to create the Mandate System which has now been replaced by the Trusteeship System.

In a *constitutional* respect the principle means a right for each state freely to choose the form of government under which it desires to live. Consistency would then demand that the majority should have the right to choose dictatorship and despotism too. That, however, would be at variance with the respect for human rights and the fundamental human freedoms which it is the duty of the organization to promote. The principle must therefore presumably be limited in accordance herewith, cf. the Universal Declaration of Human Rights of December 10, 1948, Article 21 (3):

> "The will of the people shall be the basis of the authority of government; this will shall be expressed in periodic and genuine elections which shall be by universal and equal suffrage, and shall be held by secret vote or by equivalent free voting procedures."

Chapter 2

THE MAINTENANCE OF PEACE

If we follow the scheme set forth in the preceding chapter, the primary function of the United Nations is the police function towards the maintenance of peace. It is primary in the sense that it is the most "superficial" and palpable function whose object is by effective coercive measures to combat an actual breach of the peace, or to remove the threat of such, i. e. the imminent danger of a breach of the peace.

Before we proceed to a detailed account of the rules relating to this it will be convenient, in order to draw attention to the leading ideas of the system, to make one or two comparisons with the corresponding arrangement under the Covenant of the League of Nations. It must be emphasized, however, that the comparision applies to the arrangement as originally established by the Covenant itself. In practice several modifications were introduced, approximating the system now established by the Charter of the United Nations.

Comparison with the Covenant: Organized, not merely Automatic Co-operation.

In order to make clear the difference between the two systems I will begin by exemplifying how co-operation for the safeguarding of common interests may be conceived to take three different forms, representing three stages of unity.

Suppose that the inhabitants of a densely wooded district

wish to co-operate for the purpose of combating the risk of forest fires.

This may be done by an agreement making it the duty of each person under definitely detailed circumstances (e. g. when a fire has broken out), to take certain steps already agreed upon (e. g. to come with fire-extinguishing appliances, to allow access to his land and the like). I will call this type of co-operation *automatic* co-operation, because it comes into operation of itself, i. e. without the intervention of an organ which authoritatively decides when and how each member is to act. Each acts on his own initiative, and it is necessary therefore that both the conditions and the nature of his duty shall be definitely established in the agreement. If a fire council is established, its only function is to give advice and make suggestions with regard to the performance of the duties. The rules concerning adoption of resolutions in the council are thus of minor importance.

But it may also be supposed that the co-operation is extended so that a fire council is established which, when occasion arises, has authority to decide what each is to do. I will call this *organized co-operation*, because decisions as to what is to be done are made jointly through an organ, even if the execution is still left to the individual members with the fire-extinguishing appliances etc. at their disposal. The decision is a joint decision but the action is not collective. In this case the agreement establishes no other precept for the conduct of the individual members than that they must obey the commands of the council. On the other hand, the rules as to how resolutions are to be passed in the council become of decisive importance.

Finally, it may be that the co-operation is extended to the work of extinguishing the fire. A regular fire brigade is established, which not only determines what is to be done but also carries out the work with appliances procured by the common means and with men directly under the authority of the fire council. I will call this highest type *institutionalized joint action.*

If now we apply these typical concepts to co-operation for the maintenance of peace in international organizations, the first type corresponds to the arrangement under the Covenant, the second type to the system of the UN, while the third type denotes an ideal not yet attained.

For under the Covenant of the League the arrangement was that the sanctions under Article 16 should automatically come into operation under the circumstances detailed in Articles 12—15. It was for each member to decide when these circumstances were present and then to act on his own initiative. The Council of the League could make no binding decisions, nor direct sanctions, or on any point add to the duties established by the Covenant. At most is could give advice and make suggestions, and it was then of minor importance that resolutions could only be passed if unanimous.

Under the Charter of the United Nations, on the other hand, it is the Security Council which decides whether there is a breach of or a threat to the peace and which then with binding force for all — Articles 24 and 25 — decides what steps are to be taken and by whom. Thus the Charter contains no precepts directly binding the members to use coercive measures in a given case. Everything depends on the decision of the Council. For this reason it has been a compelling necessity to abandon the unanimity principle which would entirely paralyze the Council's power of action. But in order to safeguard the great powers which will have to bear the main responsibility for the maintenance of peace, the rule of a qualified majority and the veto of the great powers has been introduced in Article 27.

On the other hand, execution of the decisions of the Council still takes place through the individual states, not by joint action. No international army has been established which is directly subject to the Security Council. Thus there is only joint decision and planning, not joint action. A real joint institutional maintenance of the peace is still a hope of the future.

The wording of Articles 25, 41, and 48 shows clearly that steps for the implementation of the resolutions of the Security Council are taken by the individual states. It must be regarded as a mere misleading phraseology[1]) when Article 42 mentions that the Security Council may take action by air, sea, or land forces. The Charter has not in view the establishment of international fighting forces directly under the Council's control, and as long as this is not the case, the idea that the Council itself could take action is meaningless.

The organized decision to adopt and carry out coercive measures is in itself a considerable advance compared with the automatic and mechanical system of the League, which could too easily lead to a difference of opinion among the members in their evaluation of the situation under discussion, so that the action comes to nothing. On the other hand, the veto rule means that the UN system of action is in a way less efficient than that of the League: it is excluded at the outset that it can be applied to major powers, and disagreement among these will make it inapplicable in other cases too.

Comparison with Covenant: Enforcement Action has not necessarily the Character of a Sanction.

The Covenant of the League drew a distinction between lawful and unlawful wars. According to this distinction a war was unlawful either on account of its aim (aggression against territorial integrity or political independence, Article 10) or on account of formal procedure (violation of the duty to seek a solution of the dispute according to certain rules and to wait for three months after the result of this attempt, Articles 12—15). In the latter case Article 16

[1]) Cf. below, note 12.

pledged the members to take at any rate economic and other peaceful coercive measures against the aggressor state. These measures were generally termed *sanctions,* which indicates that they were not mere police actions but had the character of an upholding of law as a reaction against the state guilty of a breach of law. The right thereby kept in view was indeed not a deeper substantial right, but merely a formal right under the rules of Articles 12—15 of the Covenant. For it is not excluded that a state which attacks without observing these rules may substantially have the law on its side. The sanctions, then, were measures for the maintenance of the formal rules of the Covenant directed against the party which had been guilty of a breach of these rules.

The situation is different under the Charter of the United Nations, which draws no distinction between lawful and unlawful wars. The arbitrary use of force is absolutely prohibited (Article 2 (4)). Only force used in the service of the organization plus self-defence until the Security Council has taken the necessary measures for the maintenance of peace are lawful. All armed aggression — irrespective of its aim and the procedure — is unlawful, therefore, as a violation of the Charter. But the Charter contains *no rule that action under Chapter VII shall always be taken against the combatant that must be regarded as the aggressor.* For under Article 39 the Security Council need not decide on this question but may be satisfied with the decision that there is a "breach of the peace" (and not an "act of aggression"). In that case the Council is free to decide against whom the enforcement action shall be directed. It may then take into consideration both the deeper substantial right and practical means of ending the war most speedily. It is even quite possible that the coercive measures may be directed against both parties at once. If, on the other hand, the Council has chosen to brand one of the parties as the aggressor under Article 39, it must be assumed, in accordance with the expression in Article 1 (1) ("suppression of acts of aggression") that the Council is bound to direct the coercive measures against the aggressor — irrespective of the deeper substantial right. Compare with this the fact that consideration for law and justice is not a restrictive principle in the function of maintaining peace.[2]) Hence in this instance action under Chapter VII — as under the Covenant — has the character of a sanction intended to enforce the Charter's interdict against recourse to war.

The failure of the Security Council to brand one of the parties as the aggressor may be supposed to be due to the following circumstances:

(1) The facts may be obscure in themselves or not properly elucidated;

(2) There may be a difference of opinion within the Council which according to the voting procedure prevents a resolution being passed one way or the other;

(3) The substantial legal situation. Let us suppose, for instance, that the Council in a dispute between states A and B has tried pacific settlement by recommending a solution to the advantage of A, but that B refuses to discharge its duty, and that A then resorts to war against B. A is then obviously the aggressor, but the Council would be in a peculiar situation if it were now to take coercive measures against the state whose substantial right it had itself formally recognized. Here the strain between formal and substantial rights is so great that it seems impossible to disregard the substantial basis and employ sanctions against the aggressor.[3]) The Covenant had an express rule for such a situation, according to which sanctions were excluded against a state that complied with the unanimous decision of the Council, Article 15 (6).

On this point the system of the Charter of the United Nations is no doubt more reasonable than the Covenant. It is more flexible. Even though in practice the coercive measures would mostly acquire the character of sanctions due to the formal guilt of the aggressor, an opportunity is yet left open for a freer exercise of discretion, also taking into consideration the substantial right or the factors in the actual situation.

---

[2]) Cf. above p. 117.

[3]) The same must apply when the right of the state has been established by a judgment, cf. above p. 102.

The Relation between Chapter VII and Chapter VI.

In case of a breach of or a threat to the peace it is the principal function of the Security Council to try to restore peace by enforcement action under Chapter VII. But that of course does not exclude an attempt at the same time to settle the dispute which has given rise to the struggle by pacific means under Chapter VI. Thus the two Chapters do not exclude each other but deal with two aspects of the same matter, the breach of peace (or threat to the peace) and the dispute at the bottom of it.

This is indeed expressly emphasized in Article 39, which lays down that the Security Council, under the said circumstances, shall "make recommendations or decide what measures shall be taken in accordance with Articles 41 and 42." In the Report of the Committee concerned it was expressly stated that the word "recommendation" referred to proposals for pacific settlement in accordance with Chapter VI. It is added that this will especially apply to cases where there is merely a threat to the peace.[4])

Under Article 24 it is the *Security Council* which has the main responsibility for the maintenance of international peace and security, and which also has the sole power to decide upon action under Chapter VII. The rules relating to this point will now be given in more detail.

The Initiative.

Under Article 39 the Security Council comes into action *ex officio.* But in addition there are several rules according to which a breach of or a threat to the peace can be *brought to the attention* of the Council. The effect of this is not that the Security Council is *bound* to take action for the maintenance of peace under Chapter VII. Since, on the other hand, the express warrant cannot be totally without any significance, it must be supposed that the effect of a request to the Security

---

4) *Goodrich and Hambro,* 265.

Council is that the Council is bound to go into the matter and decide whether or not there are grounds for further action.

A matter may be brought to the attention of the Council by

(1) Any member with reference to any dispute, Article 35 (1).

(2) A state that is not a member, with reference to a dispute to which it is a party, if it accepts in advance for the purposes of the dispute the obligations of pacific settlement provided in the Charter. Article 35 (2).

(3) The Secretary-General, Article 99.

(4) The General Assembly, Article 11 (3).

The Duties of the Members in their Mutual Relations.

Under Article 2 (4) the members shall refrain, in their international relations, from threat or use of force, whether against the territorial or political independence of any state, or in any other way inconsistent with the purposes of the United Nations.

Article 51, however, makes exception for the "inherent" right of self-defence, both individually and collectively, in case of armed attack against a member, until the Security Council has taken the measures necessary to restore international peace and security.

Self-evident as this exception is, it still threatens to render the main rule illusory because, as is well known, it is often difficult to say who is the aggressor, and nearly every war is asserted by each of the combatants to be a defensive war — for its own part. Profiting from unhappy experiences with previous endeavours, the sponsors in the drafting of the Charter have deliberately refrained from any attempt to define the term "aggressor".[5] If, however, the Security Council under Article 39 has branded one of the parties as the aggressor, this must be binding for the interpretation of Article 51.

The actual significance of Article 51 is not so much that

5) *Goodrich and Hambro*, 157.

it establishes the "inherent" right to self-defence as that it lays down that it can also be exercised *collectively*. This prepares the way for regional defence arrangements, by which the members — on the model of the Inter-American Treaty of Reciprocal Assistance (the *Rio Pact*) of September 2, 1947,[6]) the *Western European Union* of March 17, 1948,[7]) or the *North Atlantic Treaty* of March 18, 1949 [8]) — pledge themselves to come to each other's assistance if one of them is attacked. But there is presumably nothing to prevent collective self-defence also comprising help given without such previous agreement. This will become of decisive importance if disagreement within the Security Council renders concerted action impossible. Individual members or groups of these may then be able to intervene on their own account for the defence of the party attacked. True, it must be conceded that this involves the danger that the whole security system will collapse. If different states have different views as to who is the aggressor, and the Council also has not been able to reach a decision on this question, there is danger of an extensive war, without this being contrary to the Charter. It should be kept in mind, however, that the right to self-defence only exists until the Security Council has taken the necessary steps for the maintenance of international peace and security. As things are, this limitation will hardly, however, mean much in practice.

Steps that may be taken by the Organization.

The decisive condition for all further action under Chapter VII is that in the opinion of the Security Council there is *a threat to the peace, a breach of the peace, or an act of*

---

6) For the text see *International Organisation* II (1948), 202.
7) Text see l. c. II (1948), 427.
8) Text see l. c. III (1949), 393.

aggression. A formal resolution to that effect must therefore be passed before further steps can be taken. Here the veto rule comes into operation, Article 27 (3).

In order to establish a breach of the peace or an act of aggression it cannot be necessary that there has been open military fighting. If, for instance, a great power occupies a small country which owing to inequality of strength does not resist, such a violation is also a breach of the peace.

The measures that can then be taken under Chapter VII by the Security Council are these:

(1) branding one of the parties as the aggressor, Article 39;
(2) deciding what provisional steps shall be taken in accordance with Article 40;
(3) deciding upon economic and diplomatic measures in accordance with Article 41;
(4) deciding upon measures involving the use of armed forces in accordance with Article 42.

The order of succession is not binding in any other way than that a decision under (2) can only precede decisions under (3) and (4).[9]

Branding as an Aggressor.

This measure must normally be supposed not to be an independent act but to be implied in the fundamental decision taken under Article 39.

As previously stated, this need not necessarily be the case. If it happens, it has partly a moral effect, partly the effect of giving the coercive action the character of sanctions against the aggressor.

---

9) Article 40 further lays down that decisions under this article can only be made before the Council makes the recommendations provided for in Article 39 — i. e. concerning pacific settlement, cf. above p. 143. This is devoid of all meaning and must therefore be regarded as unwritten.

Provisional Measures.

Under Article 40 the Security Council can, in order to prevent aggravation of the situation, before deciding to take steps in accordance with Articles 41 or 42,[10]) call upon the parties to comply with such provisional measures as the Council deems necessary or desirable. Such measures may be: that the parties shall stop hostilities, withdraw their troops to a certain line, place a certain area under international control, etc. The Article has already repeatedly been made use of in practice, e. g. during the conflicts in Palestine.

Being external police measures under Chapter VII these provisions are not intended to regulate the legal position of the parties. Article 40 states emphatically that they are without prejudice to the rights, claims, and positions of the parties concerned. When it is said that the Security Council shall duly take account of failure to comply with such provisional measures, this does not refer to the activities of the Council for the pacific settlement of disputes but to possible subsequent enforcement action under Articles 41 and 42. Failure to comply with the recommendations of the Council must be taken into account in estimating a party's culpability as an aggressor, and hence also in respect of enforcement action.

Economic and Diplomatic Measures.

Under Article 41 the Security Council may decide what measures, apart from use of armed force, shall be taken in order to give effect to its decisions, and it can call upon the members to apply such measures. These may include complete or partial interruption of economic relations and of rail, sea, air, postal, telegraphic, radio, and other means of communication, and the severance of diplomatic relations.

---

10) Cf. note 9.

The expression "to give effect to its decisions" is not well-chosen. It seems to suggest that behind the decisions of the Council as to economic measures there are other substantial decisions concerning the settlement of the dispute which are now to be carried out by force. But this is not the case. The Security Council has no authority to settle disputes with binding force, and its activity for the maintenance of peace does not take place in order to carry through resolutions previously passed but is merely in the nature of a police action. The resolutions of the Security Council under Article 41 are decisions as to the use of economic measures for the restoration of peace, nothing else.

Otherwise the scope of the Council's authority is clear enough. It can decide

(1) whether or not any steps shall be taken. The phraseology of Article 39 cannot mean that the Council is bound either to make recommendations under Chapter VII, or to decide upon measures according to Articles 41 and 42;
(2) what categories of economic measures shall be brought to bear. It should be noted that the list in Article 41 is not exhaustive;
(3) against which of the parties the measures shall be directed, or if against them both, and
(4) what member states shall take part in the execution of the decisions, Article 48 (1).

The efficiency of the economic measures will largely depend on how far the United Nations will succeed in becoming a universal organization. If a not inconsiderable number of states remains outside there will be a risk that the economic boycott will merely lead to the commercial intercourse being transferred from the member states to the outside states, to the prejudice of the members' interests and the intended effect. In this connection we must, however, recall Article 2 (6),[11]) which will possibly be used to force outside states, too, to take part in the blockade. Attempts of this kind will hardly be successful, however,

11) See above, p. 32.

unless all major states become members of the United Nations.

The economic measures have the added disadvantage that the burden of initiating them may fall very unequally on the members, according to the extent of their normal intercourse with the boycotted state. A member's economy may be largely based on trade with this very state, while another member has hardly any economic contact with it. In such cases recourse may be had to Article 50. Under that Article any state, whether a member of the United Nations or not, which finds itself confronted with special economic problems on account of the carrying out of enforcement (or preventive) measures has the right to consult the Security Council with regard to a solution of those problems. The formulation is very non-committal. Nothing is said as to what the solution is to be. Since it likewise appears from Article 48 that the Council may exempt a state from participating in the economic blockade — a solution which, be it noted, will hardly be practical — it must be intended that the Council can award to the state in question financial compensation out of the means of the organization, or call upon the other members to come to the assistance of the distressed state.

Military Measures.

If the Security Council should judge that economic measures in accordance with Article 41 will be or have proved to be inadequate, it may decide under Article 42 that measures shall be taken[12]) by the use of such air, sea, or land forces as will be necessary to maintain or restore international peace and security. Such measures may include demonstrations, blockade and other operations by air, sea, or land forces belonging to the members of the United Nations.

A. Duties of Members. — While the obligations of the members to initiate economic measures under Article 41 are unlimited, the same does not apply to measures involving the use of armed forces. The problem has been left open in the

12) I use a wording here different from that of the Charter, cf. above note 1, and below where the command is referred to.

Charter, since it is laid down in Article 43 that a *special agreement* or agreements are to be concluded. This has not yet been done, and until it is, no duty at all is imposed on the members. In the meanwhile the organization must fall back on the transitional rule in Article 106.

Since the reference is to a "special agreement or agreements", the basis may, according to its form, be a joint agreement with all the members or a number of agreements between the organization and individual members, or a combination of both. They are to be made between the Security Council and members or groups of members (or all members) and are to be ratified by the signatory states in accordance with their respective constitutional processes, Article 43 (3).

This arrangement shall govern

(1) the numbers, types, degree of readiness and general location of the armed forces to be made available to the Security Council, including especially the contingents of air forces ready for immediate use;

(2) the nature of the assistance and the facilities, including rights of passage, which are to be given.

B. The Authority of the Security Council. — As in the case of the economic measures it is also the function of the Council to decide:

(1) whether or not military measures are to be taken;
(2) of what they are to consist;
(3) against whom they are to be directed; and
(4) which member states are to participate in carrying out these measures.

As to the last point it should be noted that it has been thought right that such an important decision as that of a member taking part in a military action with armed forces should not be made without the member concerned being given an opportunity of stating its opinion and taking part in the decision. Hence in Article 44 it has been laid down that the Council, before imposing such an obligation on a member, shall invite that member, if it so desires, to participate in the decision of the Council concerning the employment of contingents of that member's armed forces. This rule does not apply to the request for "assistance and facilities".

Since the invited state takes part with the right of voting in the deliberations of the Council, the number of votes is increased from 11 to 12, but the voting procedure of Article 27 is retained unchanged. If several states are invited, each state only has a vote in so far as its own affairs are concerned.

While an economic boycott can be carried out by each individual state on its own account, the initiation of military action, on the contrary, requires mutual co-ordination according to a common plan. The Council has therefore in this case further authority

(5) to give instructions for the carrying out of the operations, i. e. to undertake the *strategic direction* of all operations.

In the preparation of such plans for the use of armed forces the Council is assisted by the Military Staff Committee,[13]) Article 46. Any member not permanently represented on the Committee shall be invited by the latter to be associated with it when the efficient discharge of the Committee's responsibilities requires the participation of that member in its work.

The Military Staff Committee shall be responsible under the Security Council for the strategic direction of all armed forces placed at the disposal of the Council, Article 47 (3).

As to the *command* of the forces it is laid down in Article 47 (3) that this question is to be worked out later, while in Article 47 (1) it seems to be implied that the command is with the Council (the Committee). These somewhat vague provisions cannot, however, alter the conception in principle. As long as the armed forces employed are national forces, as assumed at the end of Article 42, the command must, according to the definition, be national. The soldier then owes allegiance to his national superiors alone, and is only liable to punishment under the national military code. The intention can at most be that the members in

---

13) Above p. 87.

the contemplated later arrangement are to undertake international obligations by delegating the command to the Council. But even in that case the command is and will remain national in the last instance, as surely as a breach of this obligation can only entail international effects for the state and does not affect the national duty of obedience. The individual soldier will be liable to punishment only for failing to obey his national superiors.

The facts may then be described as follows. The Council (Committee) has the supreme strategic direction, and works out binding common plans for carrying out the operations. This takes place through the medium of the national command. The establishment of a common supreme command is contemplated but the order to march given even by this is only internationally binding, and therefore in order to be made binding on the soldiers must be explicitly or tacitly endorsed by the national command. A genuine international army or "foreign legion", i. e. a legion whose soldiers are bound to obey the Security Council directly, has not been envisaged in the Charter. The United Nations have not the character of a federal state with its own military forces under the immediate authority of the organization.

The Position of the General Assembly.

Chapter VII only mentions the Security Council as competent to decide upon enforcement action for the maintenance of peace.

Since resolutions passed in the General Assembly — apart from organizational affairs — can never have any higher degree of authority than that of recommendation, it follows that the General Assembly will never be able to pass binding resolutions under Chapter VII.

A question which may become of the greatest practical importance, owing to the way relations between the Council and the General Assembly have developed, is whether the General Assembly will be able to exercise a *similar function by making recommendations* not only to the Security Council but directly to the individual members calling for enforcement actions. If this can be done it will be possible in this way — in spite of resistance in the Security Council with its veto right — to initiate measures and legitimize actions which would otherwise be unlawful, possibly as a war of aggression according to Article 2 (4).[14])

It now follows clearly from Article 12 (1) that nothing of the kind can happen as long as the Security Council is exercising in respect of the dispute in question the functions assigned to it in the Charter. The question is then narrowed down to the cases in which the Council is not exercising its functions.

Even though it was originally scarcely the intention that the General Assembly should exercise any function of this kind, there is, on the other hand, hardly anything in the Charter to prevent it. This would only crown a trend towards the political influence of the General Assembly, already far advanced and due to paralysis of the activities of the Security Council because of the veto right and its application.

The only provision which may give rise to doubts is the statement in Article 11 (2) that the General Assembly shall refer every question necessitating action to the Security Council, either before or after discussion.

This provision may be understood to mean that recommendations on such questions by the General Assembly are excluded. In support of this interpretation it may be pointed out that it would otherwise be superfluous.

A normal reading, however, would seem to favour the interpretation that the provision is *ex tuto.* Article 11 (2)

---

14) This co-ordinates and is supplementary to the right of collective self-defence, referred to above p. 145.

deals with the competence of the General Assembly in political questions, and is composed of three stages. First, the Assembly can *discuss* such questions; then (except as provided in Article 12) it may make *recommendations.* Finally comes the passage dealt with here. There is nothing to indicate that it has the character of a restriction on the right to make recommendations. Hence it would seem most natural to regard it as relating to a *third stage,* beyond both "discussion" and "recommendation", namely that of binding resolutions under Chapter VII. At any rate nothing to the contrary can be inferred from the addition "before or after discussion". For it would be excluded to add "or before or after recommendations have been made," since Article 12 (1) excludes the making of recommendations after the matter has been referred to the Council.

If this solution is accepted it will be of decisive importance to establish the scope of the reservation as to the exclusive competence of the Council under Article 12 (1). The Council must satisfy the condition that it "is exercising the functions assigned to it in the present Charter." The question is whether this condition is satisfied once the matter has been placed on the agenda of the Council or whether it is further required that the Council should occupy itself more directly with it. The technical need of a sharp criterion will, I think, compel us to abide by the former possibility: as long as the matter is on the agenda of the Council the General Assembly is excluded from making recommendations.[15]) Then another important point will arise. According to what rules of voting is it to be decided whether a question shall remain on or be removed from the agenda of the Council? In practice it has been accepted that the decision is procedural, so that the veto rule does not come into operation.[16]) This is of the greatest significance. The result is that a single great power cannot prevent the General Assembly from taking up the matter in accordance with the above, and making recommendations on initiation of enforcement action under Chapter VII.

---

15) Otherwise *Goodrich and Hambro,* 169; *Evatt,* The United Nations, 123.

16) S. C. Off. Rec. 2. year 2401—2405.

Chapter 3

THE PACIFIC SETTLEMENT OF DISPUTES

Among the functions designed to prevent war must first be mentioned that of settling disputes, which is aimed against the external and tangible causes of war.

At this point the *International Court* has its special role, but only within a limited field. Firstly, a decision by the Court is only a really appropriat means of settlement as far as legal disputes are concerned, and most of the conflicts which may lead to war are not of this character. Secondly, submission to the jurisdiction of the Court has not been made obligatory by the Charter but in all cases assumes a special arrangement. More extensive measures for the settlement of disputes are therefore necessary, particularly with a view to political disputes.

For that function too the Charter has assigned the main responsibility to the Security Council. Chapter VI, which contains the detailed rules concerning settlement, only mentions the Court incidentally.

The Flaws of the System.

It might have been expected that a strong authority had been assigned to the Security Council on this point so as to strengthen the peace in the world by making the Council a universal arbitral tribunal which could authoritatively settle all political disputes. By this means the Security Council might become that organ of peaceful adjustment of which the world is so greatly in need owing to the static character of international law.

That, however, is by no means the case. If we compare Chapter VI with Chapter VII, we are struck by the remarkable weakness of the content of Chapter VI.

In the first place the Security Council has in no case any authority to settle a dispute with binding force. Hence it can never exercise any activities having the character of (political) arbitration, but at most make non-binding recommendations, i. e. mediate.

Secondly, the Council has no independent right to this limited activity. Under Article 37 it can only do so when the parties — or one of them — submit the matter to the Council. Only when there is a threat to the peace so that recourse can be had to Article 39 can the Council make recommendations even if the parties have not called upon it for assistance.

Thirdly, it might at any rate be expected that parties calling upon the Council might demand that the Council make an attempt to settle the conflict by making a recommendation for its solution. For this would seem to be the logical counterpart of the categorical interdict against the parties themselves resorting to force, Article 2 (4). This is indeed the case within the state. As a counterpart to the interdict against citizens exercising their own justice there is the right for them to have their disputes settled by the law courts and the legislative power. But under the Charter the Security Council has no such duty. Not only may it under Article 37 (2) confine itself to recommending to the parties a course of action by which they can settle the dispute themselves (Article 36); it may even entirely refuse to take up the matter if it does not deem that a continuance of the dispute is likely to endanger the maintenance of international peace and security.

There is something strangely incongruous in the meagre

scope of the power and duty of the Security Council to bring about a peaceful settlement compared with its considerable power under Chapter VII to order enforcement measures in case of a breach of the peace. It would have been reasonable if the Charter had primarily given the Council the power and duty to say to the states (apart from the great powers, cf. the veto rule) that things must be arranged in such and such a way, and further, as a supplement to this, had given the Council power to enforce its decisions. As it is, the Council can order coercive measures to be used (or make recommendations concerning settlement) when the peace is threatened or broken, but before it has come to this the Council has no independent authority even to make recommendations for the settlement of disputes. The state, on the other hand, has no right to have its claims adjudicated. Thus the state, if its claims are not voluntarily recognized, is expected to accept passively the *status quo*. This attitude is at variance with the dynamics of progress. It cuts off all peaceful adjustment which is not based on mutual understanding and is in reality an invitation to war. Only on the threat or outbreak of war does the Council come into action with independent power to settle the dispute and extinguish the fire.

It will appear from this that the Security Council lacks all power to carry through an authoritative peaceful adjustment, or an independent power and duty even to make timely recommendations for peaceful adjustment, and that in principle the enforcement machinery always aims at maintaining the existing state of affairs. Only in so far as the conditions are altered voluntarily or by the unlawful use of force will the new conditions be accepted as a new *de facto* state of affairs with a claim to protection.

This utterly static conception of the peace-preserving function of the organization is the greatest technical defect of the Charter. It is not — like the veto rule — founded on political difficulties of great weight. A far more effective system of pacific settlement could have been established without any great difficulty. As will be mentioned below, this is only in some degree remedied by the powers assigned to the General Assembly.

It has been characterized as a great advance that the United Nations, at the San Francisco Conference, were furnished with the "teeth" which the League of Nations lacked. Perhaps that is so. But it seems to me that it would have been more important, and at any rate the necessary condition for the proper function of the teeth, that the United Nations had been given a tongue with which to speak with authority. Then it might afterwards use its teeth to claim respect for its jurisdictional power.

The Initiative.

The same applies to this as was said above on p. 143 about initiation of coercive measures, but with one essential qualification. The Council cannot *ex officio* intervene in a dispute and propose conditions for its settlement. That step implies that the parties to the dispute (or one of them) has submitted the matter to the Council (Article 37). As already mentioned, it must be considered regrettable that the Council is thus without independent powers on this essential point.

Duties of the Members in their Mutual Relations.

These are two: first the parties to a dispute are to try to settle it themselves by pacific means; then, failing this, they are to submit it to the Security Council.

The first of these duties is laid down in Article 2 (3) and 33 (1).

While the former provision is couched in general terms, the latter only speaks of "any dispute, the continuance of which is likely to endanger the maintenance of international peace and security," subsequently referred to as a "dangerous dispute." The article must then be understood to mean that the duty in itself applies to any dispute, but only as a moral duty in accordance with a *lex imperfecta*, all legal effects decreed in Chapter VI being contingent on the presence of a "dangerous" dispute. Under Article 34 it is the Security Council which is to decide whether or not that is the case, and it can then urge the parties to try to settle the dispute, Article 33 (2).

The duty of the members to achieve a settlement does not really mean much because it is so vague in its contents that it is in fact nugatory. According to Article 33 (1) members are to seek a solution by negotiation, enquiry, mediation, conciliation, arbitration, judicial settlement, resort to regional agencies or arrangements, or other peaceful means of their own choice. The choice then lies with the parties themselves, i. e. they are to *agree* about the course of action. But if they are agreed, it is unnecessary to speak of a duty, and we certainly cannot reasonably speak of any duty to agree. Hence the provision is in reality devoid of meaning. Since under general international law a state is considered bound to comply with a request for negotiation, its only effect is that the parties are compelled to try the channel of negotiation and thus are not allowed to shelve the dispute. The injunction of the Security Council under Article 33 (2) has indeed no other effect than that of reminding the parties of their duty to negotiate.

The second duty, the duty of submitting the matter to the Security Council if the parties' own attempts at a settlement fail, is established by Article 37 (1). This Article does not mean much in reality either. The contents are definite enough, but it is entirely in the hands of the parties themselves to decide when the condition, that their own attempt has failed, is filled. Hence if they agree, they can always keep the Council from interfering on the plea that they have not yet entirely given up hopes of reaching a settlement. The Council has no power to intervene on this point.

Even if the parties admit that they are not able to settle the dispute, the Council does not acquire any competence in the matter under Article 37 (2) if they still fail to submit the question to it. If, on the other hand, one of the parties declares further negotiations to be futile, the duty of submission is indicated, and that party's submission of the matter to the Council must take effect under Article 37 (2), whether or not the other party agrees to it.

Steps that may be taken by the Organization.

The decisive condition determining all further measures under Chapter VI is that in the opinion of the Security Council the dispute or situation is "dangerous", in the sense that its continuance is likely to endanger the maintenance of international peace and security. No formal resolution is required here, however. If the question is put to the vote, the veto rule — for the reason mentioned below — does not come into operation.

The Security Council may investigate any dispute or situation[1]) with a view to ascertaining whether the dispute or situation must be regarded as "dangerous" (Article 34). An actual enquiry is not necessary, however, if the Council considers it sufficiently clear from the circumstances at hand that the dispute or situation is "dangerous". According to the "Statement" the veto rule comes into operation at the decision concerning an investigation.[2])

If, according to this — whether or not an investigation has taken place or the situation has been declared dangerous,

---

1) Article 34 says: "any situation which might lead to international friction or give rise to a dispute." This hardly contains any technical limitation. As it is a fact that the veto rule comes into operation at the decision to investigate, the question is without interest.

2) Cf. above, p. 76.

or both — the conditions for proceeding are present, the following steps may be considered:

(1) an unspecific injunction upon the parties to settle their dispute by pacific means, Article 33 (2);
(2) a specific recommendation to the parties for certain appropriate procedures or methods of adjustment, Article 36 (1);
(3) a recommendation to the parties of such terms of settlement as the Council may deem appropriate, Article 37 (2).

The Council may at any stage of the proceedings take the steps mentioned under (1) and (2) on its own authority. As already mentioned, recommendations for settlement can only be made after the parties have referred the matter to the Council.

Unspecific Injunction upon the Parties to settle the Dispute.

As previously stated, such an injunction is only a reminder of the duty of the parties to start negotiations.

According to the "Statement", the decision to issue such an injunction can be taken according to the voting rules of Article 27 (2), i. e. by seven affirmative votes, no matter which. This rule would, however, be without significance, on the assumption that all the permanent members of the Council would have to concur in the decision that the situation was "dangerous". Hence it must be supposed that in passing decisions to that effect also, the voting rule laid down in Article 27 (2) will come into operation.[3]

Specific Recommendation for a Method of Adjustment.

This recommendation is not a proposal for a peaceful settlement but merely for a procedure or method of adjustment to which the parties should resort so as to reach a solution themselves.

---

3) Cf. above, p. 160.

The Council is free to suggest what it pleases, but Article 37 (2) and (3) mentions two factors that must be taken into account in the decision.

The first is consideration for such procedures for the settlement of the dispute as have already been adopted by the parties. The expression is not quite clear. Presumably it covers both the negative consideration of such procedures as the parties have already adopted and tried without success in the situation at hand, and the positive consideration of procedures which the parties have adopted under previous treaties but not put into practice.

The adoption of a recommendation under Article 36, according to the "Statement", requires affirmative votes from all the permanent members of the Council.

The second factor that must be taken into consideration is that as a main rule legal disputes should be referred by the parties to the International Court in accordance with the provisions of the statute of that Court. This does not mean that the parties should be bound to refer the legal disputes to the Court. The jurisdiction of the latter is not, as we saw, generally compulsory. If there is a jurisdictional agreement it will follow from the first consideration mentioned above that the Security Council must take this into account. The intention is merely that the Council, even when there is no jurisdictional agreement, should as a general rule urge the parties to refer the dispute to the Court.

Recommendation of Terms of Settlement.

Recommendations for the substantive solution of the dispute cannot, as already stated, be made by the Council on its own authority, but only after the parties have submitted the matter to the Council.

The condition then is that the Council deems that a continuance of the dispute is "in fact" likely to endanger the maintenance of international peace and security. As will be seen, this phraseology is identical with that of Articles 33 and 34 apart from the insertion of the expression "in fact". No technical qualification can be supposed to be implied in this. It can only have been intended that the Council should be free to judge whether this fundamental condition governing its activities under Chapter VI has been complied with, and that it is not therefore bound to abide by the opinion of the parties. In short, the Council is not compelled to occupy itself with the matter. (That duty, on the other hand, comes into operation if the Council under Article 39 (Chapter VII) decides that there is a threat to or a breach of the peace).

If, however, the Council is satisfied that the dispute is "dangerous", it shall, i. e. it is bound to, decide, whether to take action under Article 36 (i. e. recommend a particular procedure) or to recommend such terms of settlement as it may consider appropriate. This again means that the Council even in that case is not bound to recommend terms of settlement but can confine itself merely to recommending a particular procedure.

If the Council decides to suggest a solution of the conflict, it is bound by the principles of justice and international law, Article 1 (1) in the exercise of this function, cf. above p. 116.

The Position of the General Assembly.

Chapter VI mentions only the Security Council as competent to take steps for the settlement of disputes between members.

However, in Articles 10, 11 (2), and 14 of the Charter a competence is assigned to the General Assembly which undoubtedly also includes such steps — see especially Article 14. When it is laid down there that the General Assembly can propose "measures" for the pacific settlement of any situation without regard to its origin, this expression must undoubtedly cover both procedures on the part of the parties (Article 36) and terms of settlement (Article 37 (2)). It must be implied as self-evident that the General Assembly, before making recommendations, can investigate the matter and make declarations concerning the danger of the situation or dispute.

In view of the express justification given in Article 14 it is quite unwarranted to hold that the competence of the General Assembly should be excluded by the final provision of Article 11 (2), according to which every question requiring action must be referred to the Security Council cf. above p. 153.[4])

The competence of the General Assembly is in two important respects even more far-reaching than that of the Security Council.

First where initiative is concerned. The power of the Assembly to make recommendations on the terms of settlement of disputes is not, like that of the Council, conditioned by the parties having submitted the matter to the Assembly. No such thing is said in Article 14 or elsewhere. Thus the organization is not bound to remain inactive until the peace is threatened (Article 39), and thus the defect previously pointed out in the adjustment system of the Charter is in some degree remedied. But the General Assembly has not, any more than the Council, any duty to take action.

Second, the competence of the General Assembly is not conditioned by the presence of a dispute or a situation, the continuance of which is likely to endanger the maintenance of international peace and security (Article 33 f.). Under Article 14 it is enough that the Assembly judges the situation (or dispute) likely to impair the general welfare or friendly relations among nations — which is evidently a wider criterion than the "danger" criterion.

On the other hand, the competence of the General Assembly is subsidiary compared with that of the Council, in accordance with the rule in Article 12 (1). On the interpretation of this provision the reader is referred to the exposition above, p. 154, with the addition that it is only the right of the Assembly to make recommendations which

4) The opposite interpretation in *Goodrich and Hambro*, 169, this writer feels to be unreasonable and without foundation.

is curtailed by Article 12, not its right to investigate and discuss the matter.

The General Assembly too, in the exercise of its conciliatory activities, is bound by principles of justice and international law.

Chapter 4

REGIONAL ARRANGEMENTS

What is a Regional Arrangement?

Chapter VIII, of the Charter deals with so-called regional arrangements. The fact that such limited combinations of members for the purpose of maintaining international peace and security are recognized entails in some degree *a modification of the rules set forth in the two previous chapters* concerning the function of the organization for the maintenance of peace and the adjustment of disputes.

The Charter contains no definition of what is to be understood by a regional arrangement or agency. An attempt at definition at the San Francisco Conference was abandoned as unsatisfactory.[1]) The sole limitation contained in the Charter is that only such separate arrangements as are designed to promote the maintenance of international peace and security shall come into consideration. On the other hand, it must be supposed that all such arrangements come under the rules in Chapter VIII. The expression "regional" cannot require that the participating states shall be placed in a certain geographical proximity. In Article 53 (1) the expression "regional arrangement" is used with reference to mutual assistance treaties concluded between states without any such connection.

It must then be assumed that we can include under Chapter VIII:

---

1) See *Goodrich and Hambro*, 310.

(1) Agreements between a group of states concerning procedures or agencies for the *pacific settlement* of disputes between them. Mere bilateral agreements do not, on the other hand, come under this provision, since these have already been sufficiently considered in the precepts of Article 36 (2);
(2) The simple *mutual assistance treaty* or defensive alliance, i. e. agreements between two or more states concerning co-operation in the employment of force for the maintenance of peace in case of attack on one of the participants;
(3) *the combined forms,* designed at the same time to settle disputes within a group and to maintain the peace by means of force.

In practice the third form usually occurs in connection with an agreement for co-operation in the economic and social field as well, and with the setting up of a machinery for the performance of the various functions. It is the latter, most highly developed type which is chiefly referred to in the expression "regional arrangement". While a mere defensive alliance, based on purely strategic considerations, may very well be conceived to be concluded between states without any geographical connection or cultural solidarity, arrangements comprising wide co-operation in the economic, social, cultural, jurisdictional, and military spheres will in practice only be concluded among states which have historical and cultural affinities and which are geographically connected. But even though the regional arrangement, as found most often in practice, includes co-operation in non-political fields too, it is in the context here dealt with only the activity for the settlement of disputes and the maintenance of peace that comes under consideration.

Regional arrangements may be so elaborately developed in a technical and organizational respect that they in fact come to constitute a miniature "United Nations". That is the case for instance with the *Organization of American States* founded by the Bogota Charter of April

29, 1948.[2]) In this way a systematic organization of the American states has been created which has replaced the loose mechanism existing before. Its aims are as high as those of the United Nations, and a highly developed apparatus has been evolved.

In addition to co-operation in economic, social, and cultural fields the organization aims at the peaceful adjustment of all disputes between the parties and collective security against attack.

The adjustment system is worked out in a special treaty, the *Bogota Treaty* of the same date, which is a consolidation of the eight Inter-American treaties on pacific adjustment concluded since the *Gondra Treaty of 1923.*

The collective security system is worked out in detail in the *Inter-American Treaty of Reciprocal Assistance* concluded in Rio de Janeiro on September 2, 1947.[3]) Its chief provision lays down that an armed attack on the part of any state on an American state shall be regarded as an attack on all American states, and that each of the parties therefore undertakes to assist in resisting the attack by exercising the natural right of individual and collective self-defence recognized in Article 51 of the United Nations' Charter. Each party, however, decides for itself what measures it will take in discharging its duties.

The chief organs of the organization are the *Inter-American Conference* (supreme organ, regular meetings every five years), the *Meeting of Consultation of Ministers of Foreign Affairs,* and the *Council,* which may in some degree be said to correspond to the General Assembly, the Security Council, and the Economic and Social Council respectively within the UN. Under the Council are the *Inter-American Economic and Social Council,* the *Inter-American Council of Jurists,* and the *Inter-American Cultural Council.*

The *Pan-American Union* is the central and permanent organ and general secretariat of the organization.

The aim of the specialized conferences and the specialized organizations is to treat a number of special technical matters.

Though in less degree the *Arab League* too,[4]) created on March 27, 1944 by Egypt, Syria, Iraq, Lebanon, Transjordan, Saudi Arabia and Yemen, the *Western European Union*[5]) created on March 17, 1948 by Belgium, France, Holland, Luxemburg, and the United Kingdom and

---

[2]) Text see *Intern. Organisation* II (1948) 586.

[3]) Text see l. c. II (1948) 202.

[4]) Text see *Am. Journ. of Intern. Law,* 39 (1945) Doc. sect. 266.

[5]) Text see *Intern. Organisation* II (1948) 427.

the *North Atlantic Union*[6]) created in the North Atlantic Treaty of March 18, 1949 exemplify well-developed regional arrangements.

The Problem.

The United Nations form a global organization for the promotion of peace and security. The question then arises whether it must claim to be exclusive, or whether it may tolerate separate organizations with the same purpose working alongside it.

To the extent that the regional arrangements aim at the *peaceful settlement* of disputes between the members, no special problems will arise. There is decidedly no reason for the United Nations to make any claims to exclusiveness on that point. It is in fact a well-established tradition that in bilateral or collective treaties states should conclude agreements about procedures for the settlement of disputes. The Charter of the United Nations, so to speak, merely forms a superstructure over this network of arrangements, which it has no intention of abolishing but on the contrary accepts as a possible basis for the activities of the organization; see Article 36 (2) and (3).

In this respect the regional arrangements occupy no special position compared with the simple bilateral adjustment treaties. They are mentioned in Article 33 (1) among the means to which the parties to the dispute can resort for the peaceful adjustment of disputes, and Article 52 (2) provides that members entering into such arrangements shall make every effort to achieve pacific settlement of local disputes through such regional arrangements or agencies, before referring them to the Security Council.

This does not mean that the Charter imposes on the members the obligation of subjecting the dispute to a treatment which does not already follow from the regional arrangement. It should be kept in mind that "the use of regional agencies or arrangements" is not a special method of treatment on a par with enquiry, mediation, con-

6) Text see l. c., III (1949) 393.

ciliation, arbitration, and judicial settlement, but is itself an arrangement involving the use of one or more of these methods. Hence to refer the parties to some regional arrangement means nothing more than to urge them to follow the rules which they have already accepted. The idea is the simple one that the most natural way of discharging the obligation vaguely defined in Article 33 (1) of seeking to settle disputes, is to discharge the duty to do so, already undertaken by another way. Quite the same thing must of course apply to simple bilateral settlement agreements.

As regards the activities of the Security Council it is laid down in Article 52 (3) that it should encourage the development of pacific settlement of local disputes through regional arrangements or agencies, either on the initiative of the states concerned or by reference from the Security Council.

In so far as the Council appeals to the initiative of the parties themselves this is a simple application of the rule in Article 36 (2) under which the Council is to take into consideration just such procedures for the settlement of the dispute — including regional arrangements — as have already been adopted by the parties.

The only innovation is in the provision that the Council can "refer" the matter to, i. e. bring the matter to the notice of, the regional organs. This of course applies only if there is an arrangement establishing regional agencies. Nothing similar can occur in mere bilateral agreements.

The problem assumes a different aspect if the regional arrangements aim at the *use of force* for the collective maintenance of peace — whether it is a question of a simple assistance treaty or a fully developed regional arrangement in a narrower sense.

It would seem natural in itself that the United Nations should have the monopoly over all forcible police action against the nations. The recognition of separate police organizations threatens to take the supreme authority out of the hands of the Security Council and distribute the responsibility over a number of authorities. But peace, as has often been said, is indivisible, and the responsibility ought also to be so. At the same time there may be a risk that such power organizations, in opposition to their professed object, may develop into "blocs", which are, or at any rate are believed to be, hostile to other states, and in that way may contribute to add to the antagonisms in the world rather than reduce them. Finally such regional arrangements may also tend to involve the whole region automatically in war if a single member is attacked. This will be the case to the extent that they create an automatically acting system of sanctions different from the security system of the United Nations, according to which it rests with a decision of the Security Council to what extent an attack shall provoke coercive measures from the members.

The Conference at San Francisco was not blind to the risks connected with the recognition of regional arrangements for the independent use of force. That the members nevertheless agreed to it was due to the fact that the American security system was already highly developed at the time. Very shortly before the Conference the Act of Chapultapec had been signed (Mexico, March 1945), which contained provisions for collective security similar to the current ones in the Rio Pact. Among Latin American delegates in particular there was a strong desire to preserve this security system with a certain amount of autonomy within the framework of the global system.[7])

Weighty arguments in support of regionalism *per se* may also be adduced.[8]) Like all other decentralization it has the advantage of being rooted in a concrete feeling of solidarity. It is a fundamental historical and sociological fact that the feeling of solidarity inherent in narrower circles bound together by joint geopolitical interests and by affinity of tradition and culture, is psychologically stronger and therefore a more reliable foundation for a security system than

7) See further *Goodrich and Hambro*, 297 f.

8) I remind the reader that Churchill and Roosevelt originally were in favour of a system of regional organizations, above p. 18 Note 3.

the more abstract solidarity of a world-wide union. Even though regionalism, as already stated, may tend automatically to extend the hostilities, if an attack materializes, it can, on the other hand, reduce the risk of it, for that very reason. Regional solidarity will make an attack more dangerous. Especially for the small states adherence to a regional arrangement will reduce the danger of being swallowed by an aggressive great power one by one — after the German pattern. The less efficient the security system of the United Nations is — and as yet the necessary conditions for setting the military machinery in operation are lacking — the more the small states in particular will be obliged to safeguard themselves by entering into regional arrangements, alone or in co-operation with great powers.

The position which was reached in San Francisco then, was that the Dumbarton Oaks principle that regional arrangements should be subject to the authority and control of the Security Council was formally retained. Under Article 53 the Security Council, where appropriate, is to utilize regional arrangements for enforcement action under its authority, and such action must not be taken independently but *only after authorization by the Security Council.* In view of the veto rule, according to which a single great power may oppose such an authorization, this will in fact be equivalent to a very far-reaching limitation in the efficacy of the regional arrangements. But the significance of this formal rule tends to be reduced by Article 51, which recognizes the right of *independent collective self-defence.* But this will mean that all enforcement action, even military, directed by a regional union against an armed attack — from without or within — on one of its members can be undertaken independently. Thus it is only with regard to the relatively unimportant preventive measures in case of a threat to the peace, or coercive measures when there is no armed attack, that the regional arrangement comes under the exclusive authority of the Security Council.[9])

Under Article 54 (cf. Article 51) the Security Council is to be kept informed of activities undertaken or contemplated under regional arrangements or by regional agencies for the maintenance of international peace and security.

---

9) If the Security Council under Article 39 has branded one of the parties as the aggressor, this must be binding for the interpretation of Article 51 as to which party may claim the right of self-defence.

Chapter 5

ECONOMIC AND SOCIAL CO-OPERATION

With this chapter we come to that function among the activities of the United Nations which endeavours to assure the more basic conditions for peace. As stated above, this function is mainly based on the idea that war results from distress, and that the best way of safeguarding the peace therefore is international co-operation for the promotion of the common interest and the solution of common problems in the economic, social, and cultural fields. The more the individual nation prospers, the higher its standard of living, and the better its social conditions, the smaller is the chance that it will resort to war in order to procure advantages at the expense of others. To this must then be added concern for the more intangible factor implied in raising the moral standard by promoting respect for and observance of human rights and fundamental freedoms for all, without distinction as to race, sex, language or religion.

Our discussion of the provisions of the Charter relating to this function will, however, be of another and briefer character than that which in the preceding chapters was devoted to the function of maintaining peace and the adjustment of disputes. This is because of a vast difference in the Charter's system of rules in the two instances.

With regard to the latter functions the Charter contains not only a general account of the technical spheres of competence of the organs, and the degree of authority assigned to resolutions in this field (recommendations, binding decisions), but also establishes rules for the performance of the function, both with regard to the conditions under which steps can be taken and to the nature of these steps. Thus for instance the Security Council cannot at will take measures for the settlement of disputes but must confine itself to the particular measures stated in Chapter VI, and under the particular conditions laid down for each of these.

Nothing of this kind applies to the work of the organization for the promotion of international co-operation. In this instance the Charter has confined itself to a general statement of the competence of the organization and the degree of authority of its resolutions. Within these bounds it is left to the competent organ to take the steps it deems appropriate.

Nor will there be any question of competing powers in this sphere as in the case of the political functions, where the Security Council as well as the General Assembly each has its own independent authority. Responsibility for international co-operation is vested entirely in the General Assembly, and under the control of the latter, in the Economic and Social Council (Article 60). But since that Council is fully under the authority (supervision and instruction) of the General Assembly, there is no competing power. We recall the fact that the various tasks to be carried out by the Council have been widely delegated to a number of commissions or are to be discharged by the specialized agencies brought into relation with the United Nations.

For these reasons there is little to add in a legal analysis of the Charter to the account already given — in the main section on the organizational structure — of the competences of the General Assembly and the Economic and Social Council. It would be another matter, of course, if the idea were to describe the actual activities of the United Nations.

In Article 55 (cf. Article 13 (2)) the international co-operation is more precisely defined as co-operation for the purpose of promoting:

(a) higher standards of living, full employment, and conditions of economic and social progress and development;

(b) solutions of international[1]) economic, social, health, and related problems; and international cultural and educational co-operation; and

(c) universal respect for, and observance of, human rights and fundamental freedoms for all without distinction as to race, sex, language, or religion.

These bounds are so wide that it is difficult to find any domain in public life that falls outside them.

Within these bounds the Economic and Social Council (and the General Assembly) can at will make or initiate studies and reports, and make recommendations to the General Assembly, to the Members of the United Nations, and to the specialized agencies concerned, Article 62.

In particular it is stated that the Council may prepare draft conventions, although these are always to be submitted to the General Assembly; likewise that the Council may call international conferences, though this must be done in accordance with the rules prescribed by the United Nations (i. e. the General Assembly) (Article 62 (3 and 4)).

In addition the General Assembly is to initiate studies and make recommendations for the purpose of encouraging the progressive development of international law and its codification, Article 13 (1a).

For further discussion the reader is referred to our account above on p. 88 f.

The practical work done by the United Nations in the economic and social domain is manifold and varied. As examples we may mention that the organization has occu-

---

[1]) Cf. above, p. 114.

pied itself with economic reconstruction of devastated areas, regional economic planning, the world's supply of wheat, various kinds of welfare work as a continuation of the work of UNRRA, relief to needy children, white slave traffic, criminalistic problems, town planning, conditions of transport, population questions, refugee problems, human rights, freedom of information, genocide, the status of women, narcotic drugs etc. etc., besides all the activities displayed in various fields through the specialized agencies. It is of course impossible here to convey even a suggestion of the enormous extent of the work. Millions of persons have enjoyed and are still enjoying tangible benefits through this work. The United Nations has a very fine record with regard to the more immediate relief of distress in the world. On the other hand, no very great results have been achieved yet in the work of solving the great long-term problems of world economics. This is no doubt due to the fact that the main economic problems are of fundamentally political nature and cannot be solved until the political conditions of the world have undergone a complete change.

Chapter 6

THE NON-SELF-GOVERNING TERRITORIES AND THE TRUSTEESHIP SYSTEM

It has previously[1]) been explained that the function of the Trusteeship Council is not *sui generis* but merely an extension of the work for economic and social progress in the administration of colonies and former mandate areas, in so far as these are brought under the trusteeship system. In this connection the task acquires a special character, partly because the problems are coloured by special ethnographic and cultural conditions, partly because, in addition to the other social problems, special questions crop up as to the progressive development of the colonial populations towards limited self-government or full independence. Under Articles 56 and 55 (a) and (c) the members and the organization have undertaken to work for the promotion of economic and social progress and respect for human rights. It is this obligation which is given a more specific form in Chapters XI, XII, and XIII in regard to the populations of "non-self-governing territories". This is done partly by a more explicit statement of the duties incumbent on the members than is found in the extremely vague Article 56; partly by establishing for some of these territories, the trust territories, a special organ, the Trusteeship Council, whose function it is to see that these obligations are really fulfilled.

This entire arrangement is the provisional stepping-stone of a historical development away from imperialistic col-

1) Above, p. 95.

onial administration, which regarded the colonies as property for exploitation in the mother country's own interest, towards a conception of administration as a trust under international responsibility. This evolution began with the struggle against slavery and the slave trade. The Congo Basin Treaty, signed at Berlin in 1885, and the mandates system of the League of Nations were further steps in the same direction. The advances made in the Charter of the United Nations are partly that supervision over administration of the trust territories (corresponding to the mandated areas) has been made more effective, partly that for the first time all colonial government is recognized as a task carried out in the interests of the inhabitants and under international obligation and responsibility.

Various factors have contributed to this development. In addition to a dawning realization of the moral right of the subdued peoples, the mutual jealousy of the colonial powers has played its part. The mandate system especially was invented to make it possible, at any rate formally, to maintain the principle proclaimed by President Wilson that the Allied did not aim at territorial annexation. The colonies of Germany were not annexed but held under mandate. Even though we must not see the mandates system in too ideal a light, it would still be wrong to deny all reality to it as a system for the development of colonial territories towards an independent existence. It is indeed a fact that all mandates of class A have in the course of time emerged from the mandates system and become independent states (Lebanon, Syria, Palestine, Transjordan, and Iraq).

The Common Limitations of Chapters XI, XII, and XIII: "non-self-governing territories".

The limitations which the three chapters have in common is that their rules only apply to "the administration of territories whose peoples have not yet attained a full measure of self-government".

The formulation is illogical. As a logical counterpart, we should be able to speak of the "administration of territories whose peoples have achieved full self-government." Since "a full measure of self-government" must mean independence, this is absurd.

What is meant by this mistaken formulation is presumably that the territories referred to are those whose populations, because they constitute peoples in an ethnographical sense, have a moral claim, in accordance with the principle of the self-determination of peoples, to attain a full measure of self-government gradually, as they become mature enough for it.

By the words "not yet" (cf. the expressions "progressive development" and "degree of development" later on in the same article, under point (b)) it is indicated that the article refers exclusively to peoples in colonial territories whose lack of political independence is due historically to their lower political and cultural level, and not to nationality problems and claims for self-government concerning territories which are administered as an integral part of the mother country. Thus Chapter XI will not apply, for instance to the Faeroe Islands or to the Baltic states.

It must undoubtedly follow from Article 78, that Chapter XI likewise cannot apply to territories which are members of the United Nations.

Even though the definition of the concept "non-self-governing territory" is in itself both illogical and inexact, this is a case in which these defects are hardly of any importance, for in practice it is clear at the outset exactly which areas are referred to. It is then of no great significance whether or not a really apt definition can be found. In the practical implementation of the rules of Chapter XI the attempt to find more precise criteria has been abandoned, and instead a list has been made of the territories which, according to the members' own statements, come under Chapter XI. The list contains 74 territories under eight states, among them Greenland under Denmark.[2]) As far as is known, no objections have been raised in any quarter against the completeness of this list.

Establishment of Trust Territories.

Among the non-self-governing territories the trust territories form a narrower circle, to which the rules of Chapters XII and XIII apply.

The special position they occupy is not so much due to the duties of administration being stricter in their case than those generally valid under Chapter XI, as to the supervision established to ensure that they are fulfilled.

A non-self-governing territory becomes a trust territory by virtue of an agreement to that effect, Article 77.

Such agreements may concern

a. territories now (i. e. October 24, 1945) held under mandate;
b. territories which may be detached from enemy states as a result of the second world war; and
c. territories voluntarily placed under the system by states responsible for their administration.

According to this any non-self-governing territory can be placed under the trusteeship system. Indeed, the affiliation is always voluntary, in so far as an agreement is required in all cases. From the express statement under point c that adherence is voluntary we may infer that, as regards cases under a and b, there is an obligation to initiate negotiations about the question.

Under Article 79 the agreement is to be concluded by "the states directly concerned."

---

2) See *Yearbook* 1946—47, 571—72.

This undeniably obscure expression has given rise to some doubts and disagreement over interpretation.[3] Which are "the states directly concerned" in the aforementioned three groups of cases? As to group 3 it is difficult to see what other states might come into question but the state previously responsible for the administration. With regard to the former mandates we have no safe criterion for interpretation. Does the article refer to previous members of the Council of the League of Nations or perhaps to all previous members of the League? The same goes for territories which may be detached from enemy states. Under the circumstances the most reasonable solution would seem to be simply to include only the former and the future administering authority, which will normally be one and the same state. And it is in fact this practice which has hitherto been adopted — though protests have been made by Russia. The ten "agreements" in existence all cover previous mandate areas, and none but the previous mandatory powers, which are now made trustees, have been reckoned among the "states directly concerned." The result is that there has been no other party to the "agreement". Under Article 79, cf. Articles 83 and 85, the "agreement" is to be approved by the United Nations (the General Assembly or, in the case of strategic areas, the Security Council), and in actual fact the trusteeship has then been established by an agreement between the state concerned and the organization.

Under Article 81 the trusteeship agreement shall in each case include the terms under which the trust territory will be administered — these will of course agree with the general aims stated in Article 76, though they may perhaps be further elaborated — and designate the administering authority. The latter may be one or more states or the organization itself.

The agreement may designate the territory as wholly or in part "a strategic area". With regard to such areas the functions of the United Nations are exercised through the Security Council instead of the General Assembly (Article 82, cf. Articles 83 and 85).

So far ten "agreements" have been approved.[4] In one case (the Marshall and Caroline Islands and the Marianas

---

3) *Loc. cit.* 185 f.

4) Text see *Yearbook* 1946—47, 188 f., 398—400 and 1947—48, 788.

under the U.S.A.) the area has been designated "strategic". As a result all previous mandates (with the sole exception of Southwest Africa) which have not become independent states (i. e. class A) have been placed under trusteeship administration.

The former mandated areas were:

Class A

Lebanon	France
Syria	France
Palestine	United Kingdom
Transjordan	United Kingdom
Iraq	United Kingdom

Class B

Togoland	United Kingdom
Cameroons	United Kingdom
Tanganyika	United Kingdom
Togoland	France
Cameroons	France
Ruanda-Urundi	Belgium

Class C

South-West Africa	Union of South Africa
Pacific Islands (Marshall Islands, Marianas and Caroline Islands)	Japan
New Guinea etc.	Australia
Nauru	Australia
West Samoa	New Zealand

Of these all in Class A have become independent states, all in Classes B and C, apart from South-West Africa, have been placed under the trusteeship of the former mandatory power, with the exception of the Pacific Islands which have passed from Japan to the U.S.A.

The position of South West Africa is not yet cleared up. At the second session of the first General Assembly the South African Union proposed that it be given permission to annex the territory, basing its proposal on the results of a kind of plebiscite among both the European and the native populations. The General Assembly, however, expressed a doubt as to the guiding force of this vote, refused to approve the annexation, and recommended the conclusion of a trusteeship agreement. This wish has been repeated at the two ensuing sessions, most recently in Paris in 1948, but it has not yet been implemented.

Protesting that the existing agreements were not concluded in accordance with Article 79 ("the states directly concerned"), the Soviet Union did not appoint any representative to the first session of the Trusteeship Council. In the following sessions the Union has been represented.

Duties of the Administering Authorities.

These are laid down for non-self-governing territories in general in Articles 73 and 74, and for the trusteeship territories in particular in Article 76.

a. The *general* obligations towards every non-self-governing territory rest on the basic principle expressed in Article 73 that the interests of the inhabitants of the territory are paramount and that the administration therefore is a sacred trust involving the duty of promoting to the utmost the well-being of these inhabitants. This marks the rejection in principle of the imperialist system. It expresses the fundamental idea that dominion over alien populations is not an "independent right" to be utilized at will, but a sacred trust, held in the name of the international community and with obligations and responsibilities towards it. Further, the more specific precepts can be divided according as they refer to special questions concerning the development of the population towards political independence or the economic and social questions which — though coloured by the special circumstances — are in principle of the same order as the problems usually occupying the organization.

In a *political* respect Article 73 (b) prescribes that it is incumbent on the administering authority to develop self-government, to take due account of the political aspirations of the peoples, and to assist them in the progressive development of their free political institutions, according to the particular circumstances of each territory and its peoples and their varying stages of advancement.

The formulation shows some reserve. Although as previously mentioned the Charter's definition of "non-self-governing territories" is based on the assumption that their populations have a (moral) right to "a full measure of self-government", i. e. independence, there has been no desire to establish an obligation to promote the political development as far as that. An express proposal to that effect was rejected.[5]) "Self-government", as will appear from the discussions at the San Francisco Conference, is taken as a comprehensive gradual concept. In full measure it is equivalent to total independence, in smaller measure it comprises that limited independence which is possessed by a member state within a federal state or by a vassal state and, further, by mere municipal or provincial self-administrative areas which are entirely subject to the superior power of a state. The obligation under Article 73 (b) is kept in vague terms within these wide bounds and does not specify how far it is the duty of the state to carry the development. This is made to depend on circumstances (according to the administering authority's own judgment).

With respect to these political conditions no duty to report is prescribed.

In an *economic and social* respect the obligation is to ensure, with due respect for the culture of the peoples concerned, their economic, social, and educational advancement, their just treatment, and their protection against abuses (Article 73 (a)); to promote constructive measures of development and encourage research (Article 73 (d)). These precepts coincide with the objectives which are stated in general terms in Articles 55 and 56 to be the goal aimed at by the organization and the members in the economic and social field, with the addition that due account must be taken of the culture of the peoples concerned. That health conditions and respect for human rights are not expressly mentioned cannot be considered important. These aims too must come under the above comprehensive expression; respect

---

5) See *Goodrich and Hambro*, 410.

for human rights thus comes under the demand for just treatment and protection against abuse. In this domain the Charter, in Article 73 (e), establishes a duty of transmitting information. Even if this does not form a basis for supervision on the part of the organization, it may actually become of great importance and is undoubtedly that provision in Chapter XI which is the most realistic.[6])

The organization has so far received reports concerning conditions in 72 of the 74 non-self-governing territories enumerated. In order to ensure a certain homogeneity a standard form has been drawn up which in addition to the obligatory information also contains an optional section for information on geography, history, forms of government, population statistics, and civic rights. The material thus gathered is summed up and analyzed by the Secretary-General who then hands it over to a special committee consisting of the eight administering powers (Australia, Belgium, Denmark, France, Netherlands, New Zealand, the United Kingdom, and the U.S.A.), and the same number of non-administering powers elected by the fourth main committee of the General Assembly. The special committee can, upon investigation, submit proposals concerning non-self-governing territories in general, but not concerning individual areas.

b. The obligations applying *especially* to *trust territories* are formulated in Article 76. As might be expected, though they are stricter on some points, they do not on the whole differ much from the general obligations under Article 73.

Politically the object is said to be promotion of a progressive development towards self-government or independence. Even though independence is only mentioned as an alternative to self-government and thus has not in this case either been made the sole aim of the development, a shade of difference is suggested by the express mention of independence. It is of importance that the duty of reporting, which is of a stricter character, also applies to the political conditions.

In the *economic and social* domain it is a prescribed duty to ensure to all the members of the United Nations and their nationals equal

---

6) The other obligations mentioned in Articles 73 (c) and (d) are mere repetitions of the obligations generally incumbent on the members in their mutual relations.

treatment in social, economic, and commercial matters, and likewise equal treatment of these nationals in the administration of justice (Article 76 (d)). This duty, which is limited by several qualifications, does not directly affect the population of the territory but is mentioned here for the sake of completeness.

Finally, Article 84 sets certain limits on the right of the administering authority to make use of the resources of the population for military purposes.

In a number of items Article 75 contains verbal deviations from Article 73, which must be supposed to be accidental and without importance.

The stricter requirements consist chiefly in the extension of the scope and content of the reporting duty. Under Article 88 it includes the political conditions and involves the obligation of replying to a questionnaire drawn up by the Trusteeship Council — this of course makes it possible to exact more detailed and precise information. On the basis of this questionnaire the Council then has to prepare an annual report to the General Assembly.

The provisional form contains 247 detailed questions concerning the administration of the trust territories and the progress of their populations in political, economic, and social respects. Further elaboration is planned after consultation with the Economic and Social Council and several of the specialized agencies.

Supervision.

The territories placed under the trusteeship system are supervised by the organization for the purpose of ensuring that the trusteeship is carried out in accordance with the provisions of the Charter and the agreement and is not abused in the administering authority's own interest. In principle this corresponds to the supervision in civil affairs to which those persons are subjected by the public authorities who as guardians look after the interests of minors.

The supervision is exercised through the Trusteeship

Council, which normally is under the authority of the General Assembly — in the case of strategic areas, however, under that of the Security Council (Article 87, cf. Article 83).

As to the forms of this supervision the reader is referred to p. 97—98 above.

Of special interest is the right of the Council to accept petitions and examine them in consultation with the administering authority and to provide for periodic visits.

Petitions can be submitted not only by the populations of the territories but also by other interested parties. An example is shown by the petition which in 1946 was submitted by the population of West Samoa, requesting that Samoa might be granted self-government with New Zealand as protector. The New Zealand government submitted the petition to the Trusteeship Council with the request that the Council cause an enquiry to be made on the spot. This took place in 1947 through a delegated commission which submitted a report. At the same time the government itself continued the negotiations with the population and on its own initiative carried through a programme of reforms which came near to the proposal of the report. The Council declared itself satified with this and recommended further encouragement of the population to take part in the administration with a full measure of independence as its objective, as soon as it should be able to undertake that responsibility.

In 1947 funds were appropriated in the budget of the organization to enable the Trusteeship Council to provide for regular annual visits to trust territories. The first visit according to this programme was made in 1948 by a four-man mission to Tanganyika under British administration and Ruanda-Urundi under Belgian administration. The mission travelled through these territories for nine weeks with unlimited opportunities for gathering information of every kind. On the basis of this it made a report to the Trusteeship Council with various proposals for reforms.[7]

[7]) See *Bulletin* VI (1949) 82 f.

Conclusion

GENERAL LEGAL CHARACTERIZATION OF THE UNITED NATIONS

Problems of Method.

It was a stock item of the programme in scholarly treatments of the League of Nations to round off the exposition with a discussion on the "juridical nature" of the League. This usually included the query as to whether the organization was in its "nature" a federal state, a federation, or an administrative union; whether it came under some other known type of legal relation between states, or perhaps had to be regarded as something quite different, an organization *sui generis.* Ingenious arguments have been brought to bear on this question, and there is reason to believe that something similar will take place in the case of the United Nations. The value of such discussions, however, has not been equal to the amount of energy expended upon them. This is because there has been an exaggerated idea of the scope and importance of the problem.

It seems natural to ask: when the juridical basis, the structure and functions of the organization have been accounted for, when all details have been treated, and the various problems of interpretation dealt with, what further legitimate tasks can remain for the jurisprudential exposition?

The reply is that it may be of a certain scientific interest not only to consider the existing legal relationships in their concrete individuality but also to classify them systematically by referring them to various abstract types or concepts, according to certain distinguishing characteristics. This is done too in other branches of science. Zoology, for instance, does not stop at the description of the individual animal but also seeks to classify the animals into various species, genera, families etc. This will afford an overall picture, at the same time as it calls attention to the characteristics that are essential and those that are not. For it is important that the classification (definition of the concepts) should be such as to render it possible to express by this means an interrelationship between the phenomena, a conformity to general laws. Thus, on a very superficial view it would seem natural to class the whale among the fishes because it lives in the water. But a closer study of its organism and development shows that it would be inappropriate to take this as a decisive criterion. Owing to its morphological and genetic affinities the whale must be classed among the mammals.

Similarly, it may be of interest to try to classify legal phenomena and refer them to concepts or types. It may be of pedagogical and expositional value to point out similarities and differences and to group the legal situations which have essential characteristics in common under the same type or concept. But it must be kept in mind that the reference of a legal situation to a concept is nothing but a *classification, and gives us no knowledge of the phenomenon which we did not already possess.* This fact has not been properly appreciated in the co-called "conceptual jurisprudence". There has been the belief that, given the conceptual designation, one can recognize the "nature" or "essence" of the legal matter, so that one can thereby derive a set of rules applicable to this juridical matter, as a supplement to the rules already known. Thus the definition of the concept, or its construction as it is also called, has been used as a means to a dogmatic interpretation and elaboration of the legal situation. It was supposed that once the "nature" of the legal matter had been realized this must be decisive for, or at any rate a guide to, the solution of a number of practical problems, the solution of which is not given by the known legal rules applying to the situation concerned.

This is of course quite absurd. You cannot by classifying the whale as a mammal deduce anything whatever about its "nature" as a mammal. You cannot infer, for instance, that like other mammals it moves on four legs on land. That the whale is a mammal means that it resembles certain other animals in that it has the characteristics a, b, and c in common with them. It does not of course follow that it must also have the characteristics x, y, and z in common with them. No more can it be deduced from the fact that a certain legal relationship has the qualities a, b, and c in common with others that it must also share the qualities x, y, and z with them.

The numerous doubtful questions which may arise in connection with the more detailed elaboration of a legal situation in practice, like all legal problems, are of a practical nature, i. e. they are concerned with the regulation of human conduct with a view to its importance for human interests. They can only be solved therefore by an actual evaluation of the interests at stake. This evaluation must be based on the available texts, the central ideas of the legal situation, established legal principles, and other factors traditionally motivating the practice of law. To pretend that their solution can be deduced from the "nature" of the situation, is empty formalism.

Other considerations of method must also be taken into account in the conceptual classification of a legal situation. It should be kept in mind that conceptual distinctions are not given in the thing itself but are constructed in our world of thought. Concepts may be formed in many ways and scientific research is a continual struggle to arrive at the formation of concepts which are the most appropriate as instruments for the scientific description and explanation of interrelationships. If now, in a certain field of research, it proves impossible to reach general agreement as to how the concepts should be formed, the classification problem will lose all meaning if this fact is not kept well in view. This is the very thing that has happened in the field of international law in so far as the doctrine of the unions of states is concerned. There is no general agreement as to how the types of "federal state", "federation", etc. should be defined. But if one author understands one thing, another something different by these concepts, the discussion as to whether the League of Nations or the United Nations should be referred to any of these concepts is futile. There is nothing to prevent one author from maintaining that by its nature the organization is e. g. a federation, while another author denies this — without there being any real disagreement between them. The explanation is that they understand different things by the same concept. Any general characterization, therefore, must be based on well-defined concepts.

Further, it should be kept in mind that a legal situation can reasonably be classified in more than one way. In one respect it may have qualities in common with one type, in another respect with another. It is therefore unwarranted that in practice it is tacitly implied that the characterization of the "legal nature" of a legal situation must be unambiguous. This point of view is of special importance in the case of so vast an organization as the United Nations. It embraces such multifarious spheres and exercises such diverse functions that at the outset it is improbable that it could be characterized exhaustively in its entirety as being like one of the more special types of legal relationships between states.

In accordance with what has just been said, the following three principles must be applied in the attempt at a general characterization of the United Nations:

(1) The characterization has only a pedagogical and expositional value. No norm can be deduced from it for the solution of the practical problems arising during the further elaboration of the legal relationship of the organization in practice.

(2) The characterization must be based on well-defined concepts of type and is of no value to a person starting from another definition of the type than I do; and

(3) The characterization may be ambiguous in so far as various aspects of the organization may be classified in different ways.

Are the United Nations a Federal State?

As already stated, there is far from general agreement as to the definition of the fundamental concepts in the doctrine of the unions of states, the concepts "federal state" and "federation". Here I follow the view set forth in Chapter III of my Textbook of International Law. The leading view there is that the doctrine of the unions of states should be developed as a part of the international law of persons, and the concepts "federal state" and "federation" should be formed in accordance herewith, i. e. so as to mark essential modifications in the status of the member states in the law of persons.

The type "federal state" is then said to occur when states are united in such a way that their self-government or "sovereignty" — i. e. the highest legal power immediately in relation to the citizens — has been partly abrogated and transferred to a common superior, organic system, the federal state. The decisive point is that the union has given rise to a new state which, within a limited field, possesses the highest authority immediately in relation to the citizens, and exercises this in the usual way through legislative, executive, and judicial organs. The capacity for international duties has then to a corresponding extent been transferred from the member states to the federal state. Apart from the circumstance that the concept is defined as a pure or ideal type — i. e. without regard to the fact that actual occurrences of this pattern typically also comprise a certain outward community based on the complete or partial abrogation of the member states' capacity for action — this definition agrees with the generally accepted view.

If we consider the United Nations there can be no doubt that the member states have not been united through this organization in such a way as to give rise to a federal state in the sense here indicated. None of the organs of the organization can exercise state authority immediately in relation to the citizens. In so far as the organization can make legally binding decisions at all, these always apply directly to the member states. In this connection we may especially recall that no formation of a regular international army, with the duty of direct obedience to the organization, has been contemplated.

The question put above must therefore be answered decidedly and unconditionally in the negative.

Is the United Nations a Federation?

According to the definition in my Textbook of International Law the type "federation" occurs when states are united in such a way that their capacity for action, i. e. their power of concluding treaties and having diplomatic representatives has been (completely or partially) abrogated and transferred to a common organ. In practice this means that outwardly the states appear as a unit with foreign policy and peace and war in common.

A typical example is the American Confederation under the Articles of 1777.[1]) In accordance with these none of

1) Text reprinted in *The Federalist*, ed. by Max Beloff, Oxford 1948, 453.

the member states could send or receive envoys, conclude any international agreement, or declare war, but the authority for this was to rest with "the United States in Congress assembled". Similar arrangements prevailed in the Netherlands Confederacy (the Union of Utrecht 1579), the German Confederation 1815—66, the North German Confederation 1866—71, and the Swiss Confederation 1815—48.

Nor can there be any doubt but that the question as to whether the United Nations constitute a federation in this sense must in principle be answered in the negative. The members have retained their capacity for action. No community of foreign policy or of peace and war has been established by the organization. The significance of a federation is in its relation to outside powers. As already stated, the idea is that in this relation the members are to appear as a unit because the federation acts on behalf of all. But there is no meaning to this idea where a universal union is concerned.

Often, however, the term "federation" is more loosely defined, no weight being attached to the organized community in relation to the outside world, but only to the fact that a lasting union has been created for the purpose of protecting the members externally and maintaining peace internally among the member states. On the basis of this definition it has been usual to characterize the League of Nations as a federation,[2]) and similar views have been put forward with regard to the United Nations.[3]) But even on the basis of this definition of the concept the characterization must be deemed doubtful, because the League of Nations and the United Nations as at any rate potentially universal unions cannot be orientated towards protection against outside powers — unless indeed it were against the

---

2) See *Schücking-Wehberg,* Die Satzung des Völkerbundes (1931) 83 f.

3) *Georg Schwarzenberger,* A Manual of International Law (1947) 119.

Martians. At all events it must be maintained that a conceptual equating of phenomena such as the League and the United Nations on the one hand and the American Confederation and the other above-quoted historical examples of confederations on the other hand is more misleading than instructive, precisely because in this way some striking and very essential differences are eliminated. The above-mentioned unions were directed against the outside world and were based on a common foreign policy and consequently abrogated the members' own capacity for action, whereas none of these features are seen in the universal unions.

Once it has been established that in the main the United Nations is obviously different from a federation because the organization does not concern itself with the foreign policy of its members, we can, nevertheless, on a closer analysis, point out that the organization possesses a certain, though somewhat limited, power to act on behalf of all. Thus under Articles 4 and 35 it can receive promises from non-member states that they will comply with obligations in accordance with the Charter. Under Article 43 the Security Council can conclude agreements with members concerning the military contingents they are to contribute towards the maintenance of peace and security. The General Assembly (the Security Council) can, according to the way Article 79 has been interpreted in practice, enter upon agreements concerning trusteeship. Even without express warrant it must presumably be supposed that the organization, within the scope of its functions, may conclude agreements with members or non-members by which these undertake obligations with regard to the organization; further, agreements binding the organs of the organization to the extent of their competence, thus e. g. when the Economic and Social Council under Article 63 enters upon agreements with the specialized agencies as to conditions of co-operation. On the other hand, it is ruled out that the organization should be able to conclude agreements pledging the members to a certain course of action.

The existence of this extremely limited competence can, if it be preferred, be regarded as a demonstration of traces — as the chemists say — of federation in the organization of the United Nations.[4])

The United Nations as an Administrative Union.

Administrative union is the term generally used if there exists an agreement concerning co-operation between the administrative agencies of the member states for the purpose of promoting common interests, in connection with the establishment of international organs for the implementation of the co-operative functions, without, however, having any power to take binding decisions. The competence of these organs is limited to preparing, directing, and stimulating co-operation by studies, reports, and recommendations.[5])

It immediately strikes one that the activities of the United Nations in the economic and social sphere — that is to say, all the functions that come under the Economic and Social

---

[4]) On the assumption that "under international law 'the Organization must be deemed to have those powers which, though not expressly provided in the Charter, are conferred upon it by necessary implication as being essential to the performance of its duties", the International Court, in its advisory opinion of April 11th, 1949, concerning *Reparation for Injuries suffered in the Service of the United Nations,* has stated that the Organization possesses international personality in the sense that it is an entity capable of availing itself of obligations incumbent upon its members (or other states). The Court stresses that this "is not the same as saying that it is a state, which it certainly is not, or that its legal personality and rights and duties are the same as those of a state. Still less it is the same thing as saying that it is 'a super-state', whatever that expression may mean."

[5]) Cf. *Ross,* A Textbook of International Law, § 42.

Council and the Trusteeship Council — are organized precisely on this pattern. In view of this branch of the activities of the United Nations the organization can therefore be characterized as an administrative union. It differs from the examples so far known (including all the specialized agencies) by the vast scope of co-operation. It is *the* general administrative union supplementing the various specialized ones.

The United Nations as an Agency for the Pacific Settlement of Disputes.

It is a well-known fact that states conclude agreements concerning the pacific settlement of disputes in connection with the establishment of agencies for exercising the function of settlement, whether it be by political treatment (conciliation boards) or by judicial settlement (an international court). We have then what might be called a settlement agency.

It is obvious that the United Nations, as far as their activities under Chapter VI and the Court are concerned, have the character of such an agency for the pacific settlement of disputes.

The United Nations as an Agency of Enforcement Action for the Maintenance of Peace.

The function of the United Nations under Chapter VII, for the maintenance of peace in the world by force, is an aspect of the organization to which no parallel can be found among the forms of co-operation between states before the League of Nations came into being. In so far it can be said that we have here something new and remarkable and that with the League of Nations and the United Nations a new type of agency has been created: an universal organization for the enforcement of peace in the world, not only among the member states but among all states, cf. the Charter of the United Nations Article 2 (6).

The regional arrangements which have lately come into being resemble this type in so far as they anticipate enforcement action for the maintenance of peace. But their function is limited to opposing attacks on a member — though irrespective of whether or not the attack comes from a state outside the region.

CHARTER OF THE UNITED NATIONS[1])

WE[2]) THE PEOPLES OF THE UNITED NATIONS

DETERMINED

to save succeeding generations from the scourge of war, which twice in our lifetime has brought untold sorrow to mankind, and

to reaffirm faith in fundamental human rights, in the dignity and worth of the human person, in the equal rights of men and women and of nations large and small, and

to establish conditions under which justice and respect for the obligations arising from treaties and other sources of international law can be maintained, and

to promote social progress and better standards of life in larger freedom,

AND FOR THESE ENDS

to practice tolerance and live together in peace with one another as good neighbors, and

to unite our strength to maintain international peace and security, and

to ensure, by the acceptance of principles and the institution of methods, that armed force shall not be used, save in the common interest, and

to employ international machinery for the promotion of the economic and social advancement of all peoples,

HAVE RESOLVED TO COMBINE OUR EFFORTS
TO ACCOMPLISH THESE AIMS

Accordingly, our respective Governments, through representatives assembled in the city of San Francisco, who have exhibited their full

1) The references givens in the notes below are to the pages above.
2) 116, 134.

powers found to be in good and due form, have agreed to the present Charter of the United Nations and do hereby establish an international organization to be known as the United Nations.

CHAPTER I
PURPOSES AND PRINCIPLES

Article 1 [3]

The Purposes of the United Nations are:

1. To maintain international peace and security, and to that end: to take effective collective measures for the prevention and removal of threats to the peace, and for the suppression of acts of aggression or other breaches of the peace, and to bring about by peaceful means, and in conformity with the principles of justice and international law, adjustment or settlement of international disputes or situations which might lead to a breach of the peace;[4]

2. To develop friendly relations among nations based on respect for the principle of equal rights and self-determination of peoples, and to take other appropriate measures to strengthen universal peace;[5]

3. To achieve international cooperation in solving international problems of an economic, social, cultural, or humanitarian character, and in promoting and encouraging respect for human rights and for fundamental freedoms for all without distinction as to race, sex, language, or religion; and[6]

4. To be a center for harmonizing the actions of nations in the attainment of these common ends.[7]

Article 2

The Organization and its Members, in pursuit of the Purposes stated in Article 1, shall act in accordance with the following Principles.

1. The Organization is based on the principle of the sovereign equality of all its Members.[8]

2. All Members, in order to ensure to all of them the rights and benefits resulting from membership, shall fulfil in good faith the obligations assumed by them in accordance with the present Charter.

---

3) 108, 116, 142.
4) 110, 111, 117, 163.
5) 110, 116, 134, 135.
6) 110, 114, 115.
7) 110, 116.
8) 118, 134.

3. All Members shall settle their international disputes by peaceful means in such a manner that international peace and security, and justice, are not endangered.[9]

4. All Members shall refrain in their international relations from the threat or use of force against the territorial integrity or political independence of any state, or in any other manner inconsistent with the Purposes of the United Nations.[10]

5. All Members shall give the United Nations every assistance in any action it takes in accordance with the present Charter, and shall refrain from giving assistance to any state against which the United Nations is taking preventive or enforcement action.

6. The Organization shall ensure that states which are not Members of the United Nations act in accordance with these Principles so far as may be necessary for the maintenance of international peace and security.[11]

7. Nothing contained in the present Charter shall authorize the United Nations to intervene in matters which are essentially within the domestic jurisdiction of any state or shall require the Members to submit such matters to settlement under the present Charter; but this principle shall not prejudice the application of enforcement measures under Chapter VII.[12]

CHAPTER II
MEMBERSHIP

Article 3

The original Members of the United Nations shall be the states which, having participated in the United Nations Conference on International Organization at San Francisco, or having previously signed the Declaration by United Nations of January 1, 1942, sign the present Charter and ratify it in accordance with Article 110.[13]

Article 4 [14]

1. Membership in the United Nations is open to all other peace-loving states which accept the obligations contained in the present

---

[9] 118, 128, 158.
[10] 128, 141, 144, 153, 156.
[11] 30, 32—34, 148, 199.
[12] 111, 118—132.
[13] 42.
[14] 43, 45—47, 60, 70, 78, 196.

Charter and, in the judgment of the Organization, are able and willing to carry out these obligations.

2. The admission of any such state to membership in the United Nations will be effected by a decision of the General Assembly upon the recommendation of the Security Council.[15]

Article 5

A Member of the United Nations against which preventive or enforcement action has been taken by the Security Council may be suspended from the exercise of the rights and privileges of membership by the General Assembly upon the recommendation of the Security Council. The exercise of these rights and privileges may be restored by the Security Council.[16]

Article 6

A Member of the United Nations which has persistently violated the Principles contained in the present Charter may be expelled from the Organization by the General Assembly upon the recommendation of the Security Council.[17]

CHAPTER III
ORGANS

Article 7 [18]

1. There are established as the principal organs of the United Nations: a General Assembly, a Security Council, an Economic and Social Council, a Trusteeship Council, an International Court of Justice, and a Secretariat.

2. Such subsidiary organs as may be found necessary may be established in accordance with the present Charter.

Article 8

The United Nations shall place no restrictions on the eligibility of men and women to participate in any capacity and under conditions of equality in its principal and subsidiary organs.

---

15) 44.
16) 48, 60, 70.
17) 47, 60, 70.
18) 41, 104.

CHAPTER IV
THE GENERAL ASSEMBLY

Composition

Article 9 [19]

1. The General Assembly shall consist of all the Members of the United Nations.

2. Each Member shall have not more than five representatives in the General Assembly.

Functions and Powers

Article 10 [20]

The General Assembly may discuss any questions or any matters within the scope of the present Charter or relating to the powers and functions of any organs provided for in the present Charter, and, except as provided in Article 12, may make recommendations to the Members of the United Nations or to the Security Council or to both on any such questions or matters.

Article 11 [21]

1. The General Assembly may consider the general principles of cooperation in the maintenance of international peace and security, including the principles governing disarmament and the regulation of armaments, and may make recommendations with regard to such principles to the Members or to the Security Council or to both.

2. The General Assembly may discuss any questions relating to the maintenance of international peace and security brought before it by any Member of the United Nations, or by the Security Council, or by a state which is not a Member of the United Nations in accordance with Article 35, paragraph 2, and, except as provided in Article 12, may make recommendations with regard to any such questions to the state or states concerned or to the Security Council or to both. Any such question on which action is necessary shall be referred to the Security Council by the General Assembly either before or after discussion.[22]

3. The General Assembly may call the attention of the Security Council to situations which are likely to endanger international peace and security.[23]

---

19) 58.
20) 51, 52, 57, 59—61, 68, 163.
21) 59, 60.
22) 52, 70, 153, 163.
23) 144.

4. The powers of the General Assembly set forth in this Article shall not limit the general scope of Article 10.

Article 12 [24]

1. While the Security Council is exercising in respect of any dispute or situation the functions assigned to it in the present Charter, the General Assembly shall not make any recommendation with regard to that dispute or situation unless the Security Council so requests.[25]

2. The Secretary-General, with the consent of the Security Council, shall notify the General Assembly at each session of any matters relative to the maintenance of international peace and security which are being dealt with by the Security Council and shall similarly notify the General Assembly, or the Members of the United Nations if the General Assembly is not in session, immediately the Security Council ceases to deal with such matters.

Article 13 [26]

1. The General Assembly shall initiate studies and make recommendations for the purpose of:

a. promoting international cooperation in the political field and encouraging the progressive development of international law and its codification;[27]

b. promoting international cooperation in the economic, social, cultural, educational, and health fields, and assisting in the realization of human rights and fundamental freedoms for all without distinction as to race, sex, language, or religion.

2. The further responsibilities, functions, and powers of the General Assembly with respect to matters mentioned in paragraph 1 b above are set forth in Chapters IX and X.[28]

Article 14

Subject to the provisions of Article 12, the General Assembly may recommend measures for the peaceful adjustment of any situation, regardless of origin, which it deems likely to impair the general welfare or friendly relations among nations, including situations resulting from a

---

[24] 59, 60, 81, 154, 164.
[25] 52, 70, 153, 154, 164.
[26] 59, 60.
[27] 59, 176.
[28] 175.

violation of the provisions of the present Charter setting forth the Purposes and Principles of the United Nations.[29]

Article 15 [30]

1. The General Assembly shall receive and consider annual and special reports from the Security Council; these reports shall include an account of the measures that the Security Council has decided upon or taken to maintain international peace and security.

2. The General Assembly shall receive and consider reports from the other organs of the United Nations.

Article 16

The General Assembly shall perform such functions with respect to the international trusteeship system as are assigned to it under Chapters XII and XIII, including the approval of the trusteeship agreements for areas not designated as strategic.[31]

Article 17 [32]

1. The General Assembly shall consider and approve the budget of the Organization.

2. The expenses of the Organization shall be borne by the Members as apportioned by the General Assembly.

3. The General Assembly shall consider and approve any financial and budgetary arrangements with specialized agencies referred to in Article 57 and shall examine the administrative budgets of such specialized agencies with a view to making recommendations to the agencies concerned.

Voting

Article 18 [33]

1. Each member of the General Assembly shall have one vote.[34]

2. Decisions of the General Assembly on important questions shall be made by a two-thirds majority of the members present and voting.

---

[29] 59, 60, 163, 164.
[30] 59, 60, 163.
[31] 59, 60, 70.
[32] 60, 70.
[33] 36, 45, 58, 70, 89, 131.
[34] 61.

These questions shall include: recommendations with respect to the maintenance of international peace and security, the election of the non-permanent members of the Security Council, the election of the members of the Economic and Social Council, the election of members of the Trusteeship Council in accordance with paragraph 1 c of Article 86, the admission of new Members to the United Nations, the suspension of the rights and privileges of membership, the expulsion of Members, questions relating to the operation of the trusteeship system, and budgetary questions.[35])

3. Decisions on other questions, including the determination of additional categories of questions to be decided by a two-thirds majority, shall be made by a majority of the members present and voting.[36])

Article 19

A Member of the United Nations which is in arrears in the payment of its financial contributions to the Organization shall have no vote in the General Assembly if the amount of its arrears equals or exceeds the amount of the contributions due from it for the preceding two full years. The General Assembly may, nevertheles, permit such a Member to vote if it is satisfied that the failure to pay is due to conditions beyond the control of the Member.

Procedure

Article 20

The General Assembly shall meet in regular annual sessions and in such special sessions as occasion may require. Special sessions shall be convoked by the Secretary-General at the request of the Security Council or of a majority of the Members of the United Nations.[37])

Article 21

The General Assembly shall adopt its own rules of procedure. It shall elect its President for each session.

Article 22

The General Assembly may establish such subsidiary organs as it deems necessary for the performance of its functions.[38])

[35]) 62.
[36]) 62.
[37]) 63.
[38]) 64, 67.

CHAPTER V
THE SECURITY COUNCIL

Composition

Article 23 [39]

1. The Security Council shall consist of eleven Members of the United Nations. The Republic of China, France, the Union of Soviet Socialist Republics, the United Kingdom of Great Britain and Northern Ireland, and the United States of America shall be permanent members of the Security Council. The General Assembly shall elect six other Members of the United Nations to be non-permanent members of the Security Council, due regard being specially paid, in the first instance to the contribution of Members of the United Nations to the maintenance of international peace and security and to the other purposes of the Organization, and also to equitable geographical distribution.

2. The non-permanent members of the Security Council shall be elected for a term of two years. In the first election of the non-permanent members, however, three shall be chosen for a term of one year. A retiring member shall not be eligible for immediate re-election.[40]

3. Each member of the Security Council shall have one representative.

Functions and Powers

Article 24 [41]

1. In order to ensure prompt and effective action by the United Nations, its Members confer on the Security Council primary responsibility for the maintenance of international peace and security, and agree that in carrying out its duties under this responsibility the Security Council acts on their behalf.

2. In discharging these duties the Security Council shall act in accordance with the Purposes and Principles of the United Nations. The specific powers granted to the Security Council for the discharge of these duties are laid down in Chapters VI, VII, VIII, and XII.

3. The Security Council shall submit annual and, when necessary, special reports to the General Assembly for its consideration.

Article 25

The Members of the United Nations agree to accept and carry out the decisions of the Security Council in accordance with the present Charter.[42]

---

39) 69, 89.
40) 60.
41) 52, 70, 71, 139, 143.
42) 101, 139, 140.

Article 26

In order to promote the establishment and maintenance of international peace and security with the least diversion for armaments of the world's human and economic resources, the Security Council shall be responsible for formulating, with the assistance of the Military Staff Committee referred to in Article 47, plans to be submitted to the Members of the United Nations for the establishment of a system for the regulation of armaments.[43])

Voting

Article 27 [44])

1. Each member of the Security Council shall have one vote.
2. Decisions of the Security Council on procedural matters shall be made by an affirmative vote of seven members.[45])
3. Decisions of the Security Council on all other matters shall be made by an affirmative vote of seven members including the concurring votes of the permanent members; provided that, in decisions under Chapter VI, and under paragraph 3 of Article 52, a party to a dispute shall abstain from voting.[46])

Procedure

Article 28 [47])

1. The Security Council shall be so organized as to be able to function continuously. Each member of the Security Council shall for this purpose be represented at all times at the seat of the Organization.
2. The Security Council shall hold periodic meetings at which each of its members may, if it so desires, be represented by a member of the government or by some other specially designated representative.
3. The Security Council may hold meetings at such places other than the seat of the Organization, as in its judgment will best facilitate its work.

Article 29

The Security Council may establish such subsidiary organs as it deems necessary for the performance of its functions.

---

43) 87.
44) 21, 38, 39, 45, 70—85, 139, 151.
45) 79, 80, 82, 83, 85, 161.
46) 82, 83, 85, 102, 131, 146.
47) 86.

Article 30

The Security Council shall adopt its own rules of procedure, including the method of selecting its President.

Article 31

Any Member of the United Nations which is not a member of the Security Council may participate, without vote, in the discussion of any question brought before the Security Council whenever the latter considers that the interests of that Member are specially affected.[48)]

Article 32

Any Member of the United Nations which is not a member of the Security Council or any state which is not a Member of the United Nations, if it is a party to a dispute under consideration by the Security Council, shall be invited to participate, without vote, in the discussion relating to the dispute. The Security Council shall lay down such conditions as it deems just for the participation of a state which is not a Member of the United Nations.[49)]

CHAPTER VI
PACIFIC SETTLEMENT OF DISPUTES

Article 33 [50)]

1. The parties to any dispute, the continuance of which is likely to endanger the maintenance of international peace and security, shall, first, of all, seek a solution by negotiation, enquiry, mediation, conciliation, arbitration, judicial settlement, resort to regional agencies or arrangements, or other peaceful means of their own choice.[51)]
2. The Security Council shall, when it deems necessary, call upon the parties to settle their dispute by such means.[52)]

Article 34

The Security Council may investigate any dispute, or any situation which might lead to international friction or give rise to a dispute, in

48) 86.
49) 86.
50) 162, 164.
51) 128, 158, 159, 169, 170.
52) 159, 161.

order to determine whether the continuance of the dispute or situation is likely to endanger the maintenance of international peace and security.[53]

Article 35 [54]

1. Any Member of the United Nations may bring any dispute, or any situation of the nature referred to in Article 34, to the attention of the Security Council or of the General Assembly.[55]
2. A state which is not a Member of the United Nations may bring to the attention of the Security Council or of the General Assembly any dispute to which it is a party if it accepts in advance, for the purposes of the dispute, the obligations of pacific settlement provided in the present Charter.[56]
3. The proceedings of the General Assembly in respect of matters brought to its attention under this Article will be subject to the provisions of Articles 11 and 12.

Article 36 [57]

1. The Security Council may, at any stage of a dispute of the nature referred to in Article 33 or of a situation of like nature, recommend appropriate procedures or methods of adjustment.[58]
2. The Security Council should take into consideration any procedures for the settlement of the dispute which have already been adopted by the parties.[59]
3. In making recommendations under this Article the Security Council should also take into consideration that legal disputes should as a general rule be referred by the parties to the International Court of Justice in accordance with the provisions of the Statute of the Court.[60]

Article 37 [61]

1. Should the parties to a dispute of the nature referred to in Article 33 fail to settle it by the means indicated in that Article, they shall refer it to the Security Council.[62]

---

53) 159—161.
54) 104, 196.
55) 144.
56) 144.
57) 78, 162, 163.
58) 78, 161.
59) 78, 167, 169, 170.
60) 169.
61) 156, 158, 159.
62) 128.

2. If the Security Council deems that the continuance of the dispute is in fact likely to endanger the maintenance of international peace and security, it shall decide whether to take action under Article 36 or to recommend such terms of settlement as it may consider appropriate.[63)]

Article 38

Without prejudice to the provisions of Articles 33 to 37, the Security Council may, if all the parties to any dispute so request, make recommendations to the parties with a view to a pacific settlement of the dispute.

CHAPTER VII

ACTION WITH RESPECT TO THREATS TO THE PEACE, BREACHES OF THE PEACE, AND ACTS OF AGGRESSION

Article 39

The Security Council shall determine the existence of any threat to the peace, breach of the peace, or act of aggression and shall make recommendations, or decide what measures shall be taken in accordance with Articles 41 and 42, to maintain or restore international peace and security.[64)]

Article 40

In order to prevent an aggravation of the situation, the Security Council may, before making the recommendations or deciding upon the measures provided for in Article 39, call upon the parties concerned to comply with such provisional measures as it deems necessary or desirable. Such provisional measures shall be without prejudice to the rights, claims, or position of the parties concerned. The Security Council shall duly take account of failure to comply with such provisional measures.[65)]

Article 41

The Security Council may decide what measures not involving the use of armed force are to be employed to give effect to its decisions, and it may call upon the Members of the United Nations to apply such

---

63) 156, 160—163.
64) 77, 141, 143, 144, 146, 148, 156, 163, 164, 173
65) 70, 146, 147.

measures. These may include complete or partial interruption of economic relations and of rail, sea, air, postal, telegraphic, radio, and other means of communication, and the severance of diplomatic relations.[66]

Article 42

Should the Security Council consider that measures provided for in Article 41 would be inadequate or have proved to be inadequate, it may take such action by air, sea, or land forces as may be necessary to maintain or restore international peace and security. Such action may include demonstrations, blockade, and other operations by air, sea, or land forces of Members of the United Nations.[67]

Article 43 [68]

1. All Members of the United Nations, in order to contribute to the maintenance of international peace and security, undertake to make available to the Security Council, on its call and in accordance with a special agreement or agreements, armed forces, assistance, and facilities, including rights of passage, necessary for the purpose of maintaining international peace and security.
2. Such agreement or agreements shall govern the numbers and types of forces, their degree of readiness and general location, and the nature of the facilities and assistance to be provided.
3. The agreement or agreements shall be negotiated as soon as possible on the initiative of the Security Council. They shall be concluded between the Security Council and Members or between the Security Council and groups of Members and shall be subject to ratification by the signatory states in accordance with their respective constitutional processes.[69]

Article 44

When the Security Council has decided to use force it shall, before calling upon a Member not represented on it to provide armed forces in fulfillment of the obligations assumed under Article 43, invite that Member, if the Member so desires, to participate in the decisions of the Security Council concerning the employment of contingents of that Member's armed forces.[70]

---

66) 70, 77, 140, 143, 146, 149.
67) 142, 143, 146—149, 151.
68) 150, 196.
69) 150.
70) 70, 150.

Article 45

In order to enable the United Nations to take urgent military measures. Members shall hold immediately available national air-force contingents for combined international enforcement action. The strength and degree of readiness of these contingents and plans for their combined action shall be determined, within the limits laid down in the special agreement or agreements referred to in Article 43, by the Security Council with the assistance of the Military Staff Committee.

Article 46

Plans for the application of armed force shall be made by the Security Council with the assistance of the Military Staff Committee.[71)]

Article 47 [72)]

1. There shall be established a Military Staff Committee to advise and assist the Security Council on all questions relating to the Security Council's military requirements for the maintenance of international peace and security, the employment and command of forces placed at its disposal, the regulation of armaments, and possible disarmament.[73)]

2. The Military Staff Committee shall consist of the Chiefs of Staff of the permanent members of the Security Council or their representatives. Any Member of the United Nations not permanently represented on the Committee shall be invited by the Committee to be associated with it when the efficient discharge of the Committee's responsibilities requires the participation of that Member in its work.

3. The Military Staff Committee shall be responsible under the Security Council for the strategic direction of any armed forces placed at the disposal of the Security Council. Questions relating to the command of such forces shall be worked out subsequently.[74)]

4. The Military Staff Committee, with the authorization of the Security Council and after consultation with appropriate regional agencies, may establish regional subcommittees.

Article 48 [75)]

1. The action required to carry out the decisions of the Security Council for the maintenance of international peace and security shall

---

71) 151.
72) 87.
73) 151.
74) 151.
75) 70, 140, 149.

bee taken by all the Members of the United Nations or by some of them, as the Security Council may determine.[76])

2. Such decisions shall be carried out by the Members of the United Nations directly and through their action in the appropriate international agencies of which they are members.

Article 49

The Members of the United Nations shall join in affording mutual assistance in carrying out the measures decided upon the Security Council.[77])

Article 50

If preventive or enforcement measures against any state are taken by the Security Council, any other state, whether a Member of the United Nations or not, which finds itself confronted with special economic problems arising from the carrying out of those measures shall have the right to consult the Security Council with regard to a solution of those problems.[78])

Article 51

Nothing in the present Charter shall impair the inherent right of individual or collective self-defense if an armed attack occours against a Member of the United Nations, until the Security Council has taken the measures necessary to maintain international peace and security. Measures taken by Members in the exercise of this right of self-defense shall be immediately reported to the Security Council and shall not in any way affect the authority and responsibility of the Security Council under the present Charter to take at any time such action as it deems necessary in order to maintain or restore international peace and security.[79])

CHAPTER VIII
REGIONAL ARRANGEMENTS

Article 52

1. Nothing in the present Charter precludes the existence of regional arrangements or agencies for dealing with such matters relating to the

---

76) 148.
77) 70.
78) 149.
79) 144, 172, 173.

maintenance of international peace and security as are appropriate for regional action, provided that such arrangements or agencies and their activities are consistent with the Purposes and Principles of the United Nations.

2. The Members of the United Nations entering into such arrangements or constituting such agencies shall make every effort to achieve pacific settlement of local disputes through such regional arrangements or by such regional agencies before referring them to the Security Council.[80)]

3. The Security Council shall encourage the development of pacific settlement of local disputes through such regional arrangements or by such regional agencies either on the initiative of the states concerned or by reference from the Security Council.[81)]

4. This Article in no way impairs the application of Articles 34 and 35.

Article 53 [84)]

1. The Security Council shall, where appropriate, utilize such regional arrangements or agencies for enforcement action under its authority. But no enforcement action shall be taken under regional arrangements or by regional agencies without the authorization of the Security Council, with the exception of measures against any enemy state, as defined in paragraph 2 of this Article, provided for pursuant to Article 107 or in regional arrangements directed against renewal of aggressive policy on the part of any such state, until such time as the Organization may, on request of the Governments concerned, be charged with the responsibility for preventing further aggression by such a state.[85)]

2. The term enemy state as used in paragraph 1 of this Article applies to any state which during the Second World War has been an enemy of any signatory of the present Charter.

Article 54

The Security Council shall at all times be kept fully informed of activities undertaken or in contemplation under regional arrangements or by regional agencies for the maintenance of international peace and security.[86)]

---

80) 109.
81) 72, 170.
84) 172.
85) 166.
86) 173.

CHAPTER IX

INTERNATIONAL ECONOMIC AND SOCIAL COOPERATION

Article 55 [87]

With a view to the creation of conditions of stability and well-being which are necessary for peaceful and friendly relations among nations based on respect for the principle of equal rights and self-determination of peoples, the United Nations shall promote:

a. higher standards of living, full employment, and conditions of economic and social progress and development;[88]

b. solutions of international economic, social, health, and related problems; and international cultural and educational cooperation; and

c. universal respect for, and observance of, human rights and fundamental freedoms for all without distinction as to race, sex, language, or religion.[89]

Article 56

All Members pledge themselves to take joint and separate action in cooperation with the Organization for the achievement of the purposes set forth in Article 55.[90]

Article 57

1. The various specialized agencies, established by intergovernmental agreement and having wide international responsibilities, as defined in their basic instruments, in economic, social, cultural, educational, health, and related fields, shall be brought into relationship with the United Nations in accordance with the provisions of Article 63.

2. Such agencies thus brought into relationship with the United Nations are hereinafter referred to as specialized agencies.

Article 58

The Organization shall make recommendations for the coordination of the policies and activities of the specialized agencies.

---

87) 89, 90, 95, 110, 114, 134, 135, 175, 185.
88) 114, 178.
89) 178.
90) 90, 178, 185.

Article 59

The Organization shall, where appropriate, initiate negotiations among the states concerned for the creation of any new specialized agencies required for the accomplishment of the purposes set forth in Article 55.[91]

Article 60

Responsibility for the discharge of the functions of the Organization set forth in this Chapter shall be vested in the General Assembly and, under the authority of the General Assembly, in the Economic and Social Council, which shall have for this purpose the powers set forth in Chapter X.[92]

CHAPTER X
THE ECONOMIC AND SOCIAL COUNCIL

Composition

Article 61 [93]

1. The Economic and Social Council shall consist of eighteen Members of the United Nations elected by the General Assembly.
2. Subject to the provisions of paragraphs 3, six members of the Economic and Social Council shall be elected each year for a term of three years. A retiring member shall be eligible for immediate re-election.
3. At the first election, eighteen members of the Economic and Social Council shall be chosen. The term of office of six members so chosen shall expire at the end of one year, and of six other members at the end of two years, in accordance with arrangements made by the General Assembly.
4. Each member of the Economic and Social Council shall have one representative.

Functions and Powers

Article 62 [94]

1. The Economic and Social Council may make or initate studies and reports with respect to international economic, social, cultural, educational, health, and related matters and may make recommendations with respect to any such matters to the General Assembly, to the Members of the United Nations, and to the specialized agencies concerned.

---

91) 70.
92) 60, 88, 175.
93) 60, 88.
94) 90, 176.

2. It may make recommendations for the purpose of promoting respect for, and observance of, human rights and fundamental freedoms for all.

3. It may prepare draft conventions for submission to the General Assembly, with respect to matters falling within its competence.[95]

4. It may call, in accordance with the rules prescribed by the United Nations, international conferences on matters falling within its competence.[96]

Article 63 [97]

1. The Economic and Social Council may enter into agreements with any of the agencies referred to in Article 57, defining the terms on which the agency concerned shall be brought into relationship with the United Nations. Such agreements shall be subject to approval by the General Assembly.

2. It may coordinate the activities of the specialized agencies through consultation with and recommendations to such agencies and through recommendations to the General Assembly and to the Members of the United Nations.

Article 64 [98]

1. The Economic and Social Council may take appropriate steps to obtain regular reports from the specialized agencies. It may make arrangements with the Members of the United Nations and with the specialized agencies to obtain reports on the steps taken to give effect to its own recommendations and to recommendations on matters falling within its competence made by the General Assembly.

2. It may communicate its observations on these reports to the General Assembly.

Article 65

The Economic and Social Council may furnish information to the Security Council and shall assist the Security Council upon its request.

Article 66

1. The Economic and Social Council shall perform such functions as fall within its competence in connection with the carrying out of the recommendations of the General Assembly.[99]

---

[95] 90, 176.
[96] 90, 176.
[97] 60, 90, 196.
[98] 90.
[99] 88.

2. It may, with the approval of the General Assembly, perform services at the request of Members of the United Nations and at the request of specialized agencies.

3. It shall perform such other functions as are specified elsewhere in the present Charter or as may be assigned to it by the General Assembly.

Voting

Article 67 [100)]

1. Each member of the Economic and Social Council shall have one vote.

2. Decisions of the Economic and Social Council shall be made by a majority of the members present and voting.

Procedure

Article 68

The Economic and Social Council shall set up commissions in economic and social fields and for the promotion of human rights, and such other commissions as may be required for the performance of its functions.[101)]

Article 69

The Economic and Social Council shall invite any Member of the United Nations to participate, without vote, in its deliberations on any matter of particular concern to that Member.[102)]

Article 70

The Economic and Social Council may make arrangements for representatives of the specialized agencies to participate, without vote, in its deliberations and in those of the commissions established by it, and for its representatives to participate in the deliberations of the specialized agencies.[103)]

Article 71

The Economic and Social Council may make suitable arrangements for consultation with nongovernmental organizations which are concerned with matters within its competence. Such arrangements may be made with international organizations and, where appropriate, with national

---

100) 70, 91.
101) 90, 92, 93.
102) 91, 101.
103) 91, 101.

organizations after consultation with the Member of the United Nations concerned.[104]

Article 72 [105]

1. The Economic and Social Council shall adopt its own rules of procedure, including the method of selecting its President.

2. The Economic and Social Council shall meet as required in accordance with its rules, which shall include provision for the convening of meetings on the request of a majority of its members.

CHAPTER XI
DECLARATION REGARDING NON-SELF-GOVERNING TERRITORIES

Article 73 [106]

Members of the United Nations which have or assume responsibilities for the administration of territories whose peoples have not yet attained a full measure of self-government recognize the principle that the interests of the inhabitants of these territories are paramount, and accept as a sacred trust the obligation to promote to the utmost, within the system of international peace and security established by the present Charter, the well-being of the inhabitants of these territories, and, to this end:

a. to ensure, with due respect for the culture of the peoples concerned, their political, economic, social, and educational advancement, their just treatment, and their protection against abuses;[107]

b. to develop self-government, to take due account of the political aspirations of the peoples, and to assist them in the progressive development of their free political institutions, according to the particular circumstances of each territory and its peoples and their varying stages of advancement;[108]

c. to further international peace and security;[109]

d. to promote constructive measures of development, to encourage research, and to cooperate with one another and, when and where appropriate, with specialized international bodies with a view to the

---

104) 90.
105) 186.
106) 184, 186, 187.
107) 185.
108) 184, 185.
109) 186.

practical achievement of the social, economic, and scientific purposes set forth in this Article; and [110]

e. to transmit regularly to the Secretary-General for information purposes, subject to such limitation as security and constitutional considerations may require, statistical and other information of a technical nature relating to economic, social, and educational conditions in the territories for which they are respectively responsible other than those territories to which Chapters XII and XIII apply.[111]

Article 74

Members of the United Nations also agree that their policy in respect of the territories to which this Chapter applies, no less than in respect of their metropolitan areas, must be based on the general principle of good-neighborliness, due account being taken of the interests and well-being of the rest of the world, in social, economic, and commercial matters.[112]

CHAPTER XII
INTERNATIONAL TRUSTEESHIP SYSTEM

Article 75

The United Nations shall establish under its authority an international trusteeship system for the administration and supervision of such territories as may be placed thereunder by subsequent individual agreements. These territories are hereinafter referred to as trust territories.[113]

Aticle 76 [114]

The basic objectives of the trusteeship system, in accordance with the Purposes of the United Nations laid down in Article 1 of the present Charter, shall be:

a. to further international peace and security;

b. to promote the political, economic, social, and educational advancement of the inhabitants of the trust territories, and their progressive development towards self-government or independence as may be

---

110) 185, 186.
111) 186.
112) 184, 186.
113) 187.
114) 97, 182, 184, 186.

appropriate to the particular circumstances of each territory and its peoples and the freely expressed wishes of the peoples concerned, and as may be provided by the terms of each trusteeship agreement;

c. to encourage respect for human rights and for fundamental freedoms for all without distinction as to race, sex, language, or religion, and to encourage recognition of the interdependence of the peoples of the world; and

d. to ensure equal treatment in social, economic, and commercial matters for all Members of the United Nations and their nationals, and also equal treatment for the latter in the administration of justice, without prejudice to the attainment of the foregoing objectives and subject to the provisions of Article 80.[115)]

Article 77 [116)]

1. The trusteeship system shall apply to such territories in the following categories as may be placed thereunder by means of trusteeship agreements:

a. territories now held under mandate;

b. territories which may be detached from enemy states as a result of the Second World War; and

c. territories voluntarily placed under the system by states responsible for their administration.

2. It will be a matter for subsequent agreement as to which territories in the foregoing categories will be brought under the trusteeship system and upon what terms.

Article 78

The trusteeship system shall not apply to territories which have become Members of the United Nations, relationship among which shall be based on respect for the principle of sovereign equality.[117)]

Article 79

The terms of trusteeship for each territory to be placed under the trusteeship system, including any alteration or amendment, shall be agreed upon by the states directly concerned, including the mandatory power in the case of territories held under mandate by a Member of the United Nations, and shall be approved as provided for in Articles 83 and 85.[118)]

---

115) 117.
116) 181.
117) 132, 134, 180.
118) 181, 182, 184, 196.

Article 80

1. Except as may be agreed upon in individual trusteeship agreements, made under Articles 77, 79, and 81, placing each territory under the trusteeship system, and until such agreements have been concluded, nothing in this Chapter shall be construed in or of itself to alter in any manner the rights whatsoever of any states or any peoples or the terms of existing international instruments to which Members of the United Nations may respectively be parties.

2. Paragraph 1 of this Article shall not be interpreted as giving grounds for delay or postponement of the negotiation and conclusion of agreements for placing mandated and other territories under the trusteeship system as provided for in Article 77.

Article 81

The trusteeship agreement shall in each case include the terms under which the trust territory will be administered and designate the authority which will exercise the administration of the trust territory. Such authority, hereinafter called the administering authority, may be one or more states or the Organization itself.[119]

Article 82

There may be designated, in any trusteeship agreement, a strategic area or areas which may include part or all of the trust territory to which the agreement applies, without prejudice to any special agreement or agreements made under Article 43.[120]

Article 83 [121]

1. All functions of the United Nations relating to strategic areas, including the approval of the terms of the trusteeship agreements and of their alteration or amendment, shall be exercised by the Security Council.

2. The basic objectives set forth in Article 76 shall be applicable to the people of each strategic area.

3. The Security Council shall, subject to the provisions of the trusteeship agreements and without prejudice to security considerations, avail itself of the assistance of the Trusteeship Council to perform those func-

---

119) 182.
120) 96, 182.
121) 96, 182, 188.

tions of the United Nations under the trusteeship system relating to political, economic, social, and educational matters in the strategic areas.

Article 84

It shall be the duty of the administering authority to ensure that the trust territory shall play its part in the maintenance of international peace and security. To this end the administering authority may make use of volunteer forces, facilities, and assistance from the trust territory in carrying out the obligations towards the Security Council undertaken in this regard by the administering authority, as well as for local defense and the maintenance of law and order within the trust territory.[122]

Article 85 [123]

1. The functions of the United Nations with regard to trusteeship agreements for all areas not designated as strategic, including the approval of the terms of the trusteeship agreements and of their alteration or amendment, shall be exercised by the General Assembly.
2. The Trusteeship Council, operating under the authority of the General Assembly, shall assist the General Assembly in carrying out these functions.

CHAPTER XIII
THE TRUSTEESHIP COUNCIL

Composition

Article 86 [124]

1. The Trusteeship Council shall consist of the following Members of the United Nations:
   a. those Members administering trust territories;
   b. such of those Members mentioned by name in Article 23 as are not administering trust territories; and
   c. as many other Members elected for three year terms by the General Assembly as may be necessary to ensure that the total number of members of the Trusteeship Council is equally divided between those Members of the United Nations which administer trust territories and those which do not.[125]

122) 187.
123) 60, 96, 182.
124) 96.
125) 60.

2. Each member of the Trusteeship Council shall designate one especially qualified to represent it therein.

Functions and Powers

Article 87 [126]

The General Assembly and, under its authority, the Trusteeship Council, in carrying out their functions, may:

a. consider reports submitted by the administering authority;

b. accept petitions and examine them in consultation with the administering authority;

c. provide for periodic visits to the respective trust territories at times agreed upon with the administering authority; and

d. take these and other actions in conformity with the terms of the trusteeship agreements.

Article 88

The Trusteeship Council shall formulate a questionnaire on the political, economic, social, and educational advancement of the inhabitants of each trust territory, and the administering authority for each trust territory within the competence of the General Assembly shall make an annual report to the General Assembly upon the basis of such questionnaire.[127]

Voting

Article 89 [128]

1. Each member of the Trusteeship Council shall have one vote.

2. Decisions of the Trusteeship Council shall be made by a majority of the members present and voting.

Procedure

Article 90

1. The Trusteeship Council shall adopt its own rules of procedure, including the method of selecting its President.

2. The Trusteeship Council shall meet as required in accordance with its rules, which shall include provision for the convening of meetings on the request of a majority of its members.

---

[126] 96, 97, 188.
[127] 187.
[128] 70.

Article 91

The Trusteeship Council shall, when appropriate, avail itself of the assistance of the Economic and Social Council and of the specialized agencies in regard to matters with which they are respectively concerned.

CHAPTER XIV
THE INTERNATIONAL COURT OF JUSTICE

Article 92

The International Court of Justice shall be the principal judicial organ of the United Nations. It shall function in accordance with the annexed Statute, which is based upon the Statute of the Permanent Court of International Justice and forms an integral part of the present Charter.[129]

Article 93 [130]

1. All Members of the United Nations are *ipso facto* parties to the Statute of the International Court of Justice.
2. A state which is not a Member of the United Nations may become a party to the Statute of the International Court of Justice on conditions to be determined in each case by the General Assembly upon the recommendation of the Security Council.[131]

Article 94 [132]

1. Each Member of the United Nations undertakes to comply with the decision of the International Court of Justice in any case to which it is a party.
2. If any party to a case fails to perform the obligations incumbent upon it under a judgment rendered by the Court, the other party may have recourse to the Security Council, which may, if it deems necessary, make recommendations or decide upon measures to be taken to give effect to the judgment.

Article 95

Nothing in the present Charter shall prevent Members of the United Nations from entrusting the solution of their differences to other tribu-

---

129) 99.
130) 100.
131) 100.
132) 70, 101—103.

nals by virtue of agreements already in existence or which may be concluded in the future.[133]

Article 96 [134]

1. The General Assembly or the Security Council may request the International Court of Justice to give an advisory opinion on any legal question.

2. Other organs of the United Nations and specialized agencies, which may at any time be so authorized by the General Assembly, may also request advisory opinions of the Court on legal questions arising within the scope of their activities.

CHAPTER XV
THE SECRETARIAT

Article 97

The Secretariat shall comprise a Secretary-General and such staff as the Organization may require. The Secretary-General shall be appointed by the General Assembly upon the recommendation of the Security Council. He shall be the chief administrative officer of the Organization.[135]

Article 98

The Secretary-General shall act in that capacity in all meetings of the General Assembly, of the Security Council, of the Economic and Social Council, and of the Trusteeship Council, and shall perform such other functions as are entrusted to him by these organs. The Secretary-General shall make an annual report to the General Assembly on the work of the Organization.[136]

Article 99

The Secretary-General may bring to the attention of the Security Council any matter which in his opinion may threaten the maintenance of international peace and security.[137]

---

133) 100.
134) 102.
135) 60, 70, 107.
136) 106.
137) 104—106, 144.

Article 100 [138]

1. In the performance of their duties the Secretary-General and the staff shall not seek or receive instructions from any government or from any other authority external to the Organization. They shall refrain from any action which might reflect on their position as international officials responsible only to the Organization.

2. Each Member of the United Nations undertakes to respect the exclusively international character of the responsibilities of the Secretary-General and the staff and not to seek to influence them in the discharge of their responsibilities.[139]

Article 101

1. The staff shall be appointed by the Secretary-General under regulations established by the General Assembly.[140]

2. Appropriate staffs shall be permanently assigned to the Economic and Social Council, the Trusteeship Council, an, as required, to other organs of the United Nations. These staffs shall form a part of the Secretariat.

3. The paramount consideration in the employment of the staff and in the determination of the conditions of service shall be the necessity of securing the highest standards of efficiency, competence, and integrity. Due regard shall be paid to the importance of recruiting the staff on as wide a geographical basis as possible.

CHAPTER XVI
MISCELLANEOUS PROVISIONS

Article 102

1. Every treaty and every international agreement entered into by any Member of the United Nations after the present Charter comes into force shall as soon as possible be registered with the Secretariat and published by it.

2. No party to any such treaty or international agreement which has not been registered in accordance with the provisions of paragraph 1 of this Article may invoke that treaty or agreement before any organ of the United Nations.

---

138) 107.
139) 107.
140) 107.

Article 103

In the event of a conflict between the obligations of the Members of the United Nations under the present Charter and their obligations under any other international agreement, their obligations under the present Charter shall prevail.[141])

Article 104

The Organization shall enjoy in the territory of each of its Members such legal capacity as may be necessary for the exercise of its functions and the fulfillment of its purposes.

Article 105

1. The Organization shall enjoy in the territory of each of its Members such privileges and immunities as are necessary for the fulfillment of its purposes.

2. Representatives of the Members of the United Nations and officials of the Organization shall similarly enjoy such privileges and immunities as are necessary for the independent exercise of their functions in connection with the Organization.

3. The General Assembly may make recommendations with a view to determining the details of the application of paragraphs 1 and 2 of this Article or may propose conventions to the Members of the United Nations for this purpose.

CHAPTER XVII
TRANSITIONAL SECURITY ARRANGEMENTS

Article 106

Pending the coming into force of such special agreements referred to in Article 43 as in the opinion of the Security Council enable it to begin the exercise of its responsibilities under Article 42, the parties to the Four-Nation Declaration, signed at Moscow, October 30, 1943, and France, shall, in accordance with the provisions of paragraph 5 of that Declaration, consult with one another and as occasion requires with other Members of the United Nations with a view to such joint action on behalf of the Organization as may be necessary for the purpose of maintaining international peace and security.[142])

141) 33, 34.
142) 68, 150.

Article 107

Nothing in the present Charter shall invalidate or preclude action, in relation to any state which during the Second World War has been an enemy of any signatory to the present Charter, taken or authorized as a result of that war by the Governments having responsibility for such action.

CHAPTER XVIII
AMENDMENTS

Article 108

Amendments to the present Charter shall come into force for all Members of the United Nations when they have been adopted by a vote of two thirds of the members of the General Assembly and ratified in accordance with their respective constitutional processes by two thirds of the Members of the United Nations, including all the permanent members of the Security Council.[143]

Article 109 [144]

1. A General Conference of the Members of the United Nations for the purpose of reviewing the present Charter may be held at a date and place to be fixed by a two-thirds vote of the members of the General Assembly and by a vote of any seven members of the Security Council. Each Member of the United Nations shall have one vote in the conference.[145]
2. Any alteration of the present Charter recommended by a two-thirds vote of the conference shall take effect when ratified in accordance with their respective constitutional processes by two thirds of the Members of the United Nations including all the permanent members of the Security Council.[146]
3. If such a conference has not been held before the tenth annual session of the General Assembly following the coming into force of the present Charter, the proposal to call such a conference shall be placed on the agenda of that session of the General Assembly, and the conference shall be held if so decided by a majority vote of the members of

143) 30, 35—39, 47, 60, 62, 101.
144) 30, 36, 38, 39, 60, 101.
145) 62.
146) 36, 62.

the General Assembly and by a vote of any seven members of the Security Council.[147)]

CHAPTER XIX
RATIFICATION AND SIGNATURE

Article 110 [148)]

1. The present Charter shall be ratified by the signatory states in accordance with their respective constitutional processes.[149)]

2. The ratifications shall be deposited with the Government of the United States of America, which shall notify all the signatory states of each deposit as well as the Secretary-General of the Organization when he has been appointed.[150)]

3. The present Charter shall come into force upon the deposit of ratifications by the Republic of China, France, the Union of Soviet Socialist Republics, the United Kingdom of Great Britain and Northern Ireland, and the United States of America, and by a majority of the other signatory states. A protocol of the ratifications deposited shall thereupon be drawn up by the Government of the United States of America which shall communicate copies thereof to all the signatory states.[151)]

4. The states signatory to the present Charter which ratify it after it has come into force will become original Members of the United Nations on the date of the deposit of their respective ratifications.[152)]

Article 111

The present Charter, of which the Chinese, French, Russian, English, and Spanish texts are equally authentic, shall remain deposited in the archives of the Government of the United States of America. Duly certified copies thereof shall be transmitted by that Government to the Governments of the other signatory states.

IN FAITH WHEREOF the representatives of the Governments of the United Nations have signed the present Charter.

DONE at the city of San Francisco the twenty-sixth day of June, one thousand nine hundred and forty-five.

---

147) 39.
148) 22, 28—30.
149) 27, 28.
150) 27.
151) 27, 29, 47.
152) 29, 47.

INDEX